Creative DOLLHOUSES *from Kits*

Creative DOLLHOUSES *from Kits*

by ROBERT SCHLEICHER

CHILTON BOOK COMPANY
RADNOR, PENNSYLVANIA

Designed by Stan Green/Green Graphics
Cover design by Anthony Jacobson
Cover photograph by Robert Schleicher

Manufactured in the United States of America

Library of Congress Cataloging in Publication Data

Schleicher, Robert H.
    Creative dollhouses from kits / Robert Schleicher.
    p. cm/
    Includes index.
    ISBN 0-8019-8529-3 (pbk.)
    1. Dollhouses. I. Title.
TT175.3.S337 1995   94-25121
                                      CIP

1 2 3 4 5 6 7 8 9 0 4 3 2 1 0 9 8 7 6 5

CONTENTS

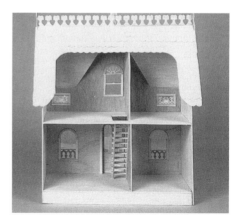

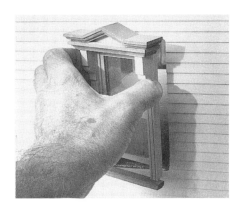

CONTENTS *Continued*

CONTENTS *Continued*

PART
I

CREATING YOUR DREAM HOME

CHAPTER ONE

WHICH KIT?

Imagine creating your own dream home. When you build a dollhouse, that's really what you're doing. Though you may start with a simple, everyday kit, you can customize it to your heart's content. When you're done, you'll have your—or a child's—dream home in miniature.

You can carry this hobby as far as you wish. Buy an already-assembled dollhouse shell, paint it and spend countless hours decorating and furnishing each room to your satisfaction. Or start with a kit and customize everything from the window locations to the chandeliers and the parquet floors.

BEING YOUR OWN CONTRACTOR

This book discusses dollhouses that you buy as precut wood kits and finish yourself. The larger dollhouse stores, however, can provide any of

Fig. 1-1. The "Seaside Villa" Victorian mansion, from Norm's, started as a bare plywood shell.

Fig. 1-2. "Lemon Twist" includes the windows, but you select the siding and shingles.

Fig. 1-3. The Walmer "Peaches and Cream" shell has been finished with clapboard siding, shingles, an upgraded porch railing and posts. The extra room extension, which provides a third room so there's space for a kitchen, dining room and living room, can be added later.

these kits assembled, usually for about twice the price of an unassembled kit. If you purchase the kit already put together, you do the rest, supplying the paint, clapboard, brick, stone or stucco exterior and finishing the interior with or without working lighting. Most of these stores will also do all the finishing for you, but the cost can be absurdly expensive. You probably want to do the finishing, if not assembling, of your own dollhouse, or you wouldn't be reading this far. . .

To finish a dollhouse, you'll use many of the same materials you would on a real house. (See Fig. 1-1 on page 3.) The dollhouse is so small, however, that your efforts can easily be classified as pure fun. Even the windows are easy to install because you can "fudge" an installation to make a window fit—even in a slightly crooked, over-size opening. On a dollhouse, you start with a substantial plywood shell, and the interior and exterior finishes are just that—finishes. They are not structural components needed for strength. (See Fig. 1-2 and Fig. 1-3.)

This book does not describe the methods for building a dollhouse from a plan. If you have the woodworking skill to cut your dollhouse from

plywood, you very likely have the skill to copy the techniques used to assemble a kit. If you decide to cut your own dollhouse, you may want to check with dollhouse dealers for plans. I suggest that you make window and door openings conform to standard off-the-shelf window and door sizes.

HOW BIG A HOUSE?

Most plywood dollhouses, as well as the available furniture and accessories, are built to a common scale. These dollhouses are 1/12 the size of the real thing. The scale is 1 inch equals 1 foot. That means that the average 6½-foot door in a real house becomes 6½ inches tall in a dollhouse and 8-foot ceilings in real life are 8 inches high in miniature. Most of the better dollhouse kits have ceilings 9 inches high.

HALF-SCALE DOLLHOUSES

The next most popular dollhouse size is called half-scale. (See Fig. 1-4.) These dollhouses are 1/24 the size of a real house. This means that ½

Fig. 1-4. Greenleaf's "Fairfield" is a die-cut ⅛-inch plywood half-scale dollhouse kit. **Photo courtesy Greenleaf Products.**

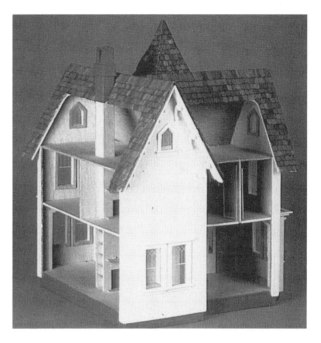

Fig. 1-5. The "Fairfield" interior includes two fireplaces, a chimney, bookshelves and window frames. **Photo courtesy Greenleaf Products.**

inch equals 1 foot, so a 6½-foot door would actually be 3¼ inches high. This is also very similar to the size of many outdoor model railroads. Those miniatures, often used as an enhancement to a garden, are featured in my *Large Scale Model Railroading Handbook* (Chilton Book Company, 1992).

A limited selection of trim, flooring and furniture is available for half-scale dollhouses. And you can find some exterior-finish plastic brick, clapboard, stone and shingle panels (mostly in vacuum-formed plastic). (See Fig. 1-5.) A few examples of trim and flooring and most exterior finishing panels are also available in half-scale. Consider getting a half-scale dollhouse if you want a fairly large, two-story dollhouse but have a small display area. John Hutt's half-scale Greenleaf Products "Fairfield" house, customized with all-new exterior trim from Precision Products, appears in the color section.

QUARTER-SCALE AND OTHER SIZES

Half the size of the half-scale dollhouses are the quarter-scale models. For these, ¼ inch equals 1 foot. The scale is very close to the one used by

Lionel's toy trains and is the scale used for O-scale-model railroads. (Model railroaders often refer to it as l/48 scale.)

A small selection of dollhouse kits and a very limited variety of furniture are available for the quarter-scale dollhouse, but a wide array of exterior-finishing panels can be found. A few firms, including Grandt Line Products, offer an extensive line of plastic windows and doors. If you are more interested in the exterior design of the miniature rather than decorating the interior, consider getting this size.

Few specific references to smaller scales appear in this book because the construction techniques are the same for the conventional 1-inch-to-the-foot dollhouse, quarter-scale and half-scale.

Also available are a few dollhouse kits and shells that match the size of the dolls in Kenner's Barbie™ Doll series. (See Fig. 1-6 on page 6.) The scale for these houses is approximately 1½ inch equals 1 foot to accommodate the fashion dolls. One of the kit makers, Real Good Toys, refers to the kits as Playscale™ dollhouses.

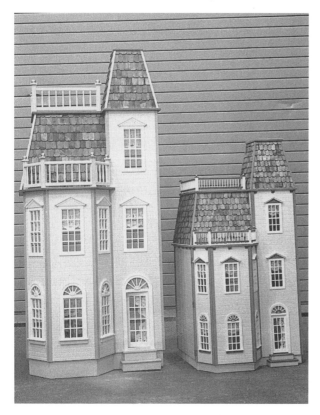

Fig. 1-6. The larger house is a Playscale™-size dollhouse for Barbie™ and similar-size dolls. The smaller house is a 1/12-scale "Victorian Townhouse." Both are Real Good Toys kits.

Fig. 1-7. Greenleaf's die-cut 1/8-inch plywood "Pierce" is 25 x 35½ inches and has six rooms. Photo courtesy Greenleaf Products.

Fig. 1-8. The interior of the Greenleaf "Pierce" has a stairway with a landing, a ladder and trap door to the attic plus a fireplace. Photo courtesy Greenleaf Products.

Fig. 1-9. Maureen O' Donnell's Southwestern-style adobe is sold as a precut Styrofoam shell.

DOLLHOUSE DESIGN

The rooms in dollhouses closely follow the scale of rooms in the average real house. The majority of dollhouses are about 16 inches deep and the rooms are 10 to 12 inches wide. To have enough space for, say, a five-room house, a dollhouse will almost always have two stories. Some of the larger kits are L-shaped to provide a bit more room in a shorter space. (See Fig. 1-7.)

A dollhouse is designed for decorating the rooms and displaying the furniture. In most cases, that means the back of the dollhouse is open. (See Fig. 1-8.) A very few kits, including some Southwestern-style houses, have open tops with the rooms arranged more like a conventional full-size, single-story house. Access to these rooms is through the ceiling rather than through

Fig. 1-10. This "Fairplay," from Norm's is a typical low-cost farmhouse-style dollhouse kit.

Fig. 1-11. "Cherry Hills Colonial" from Norm's includes right and left extensions and a second-story porch roof.

Fig. 1-12. "Cherry Hills Colonial" is sold as a bare plywood shell, assembled or unassembled.

an open rear wall. (See Fig. 1-9.) The open rear wall design, however, is common for about 99 percent of the available dollhouse kits.

COMPLETE KIT OR JUST A SHELL?

Price is a likely consideration for your first dollhouse, just as it is for a first real home. The least expensive dollhouse kits are cut, using massive steel dies, from ⅛-inch plywood. These kits include windows and trim cut from the same material, and most of the kits include shingles. (See Fig. 1-10.) Some also include clapboard siding. You must, however, provide paint and any exterior finish such as stucco, clapboard, brick or stone. Greenleaf and Duracraft are the two inexpensive brands usually found in toy stores, hardware stores and craft stores. Prices range from $45 for Greenleaf's four-room "Arthur" or Duracraft's "Lafayette" to $98 for Greenleaf's six-room Colonial-style "Jefferson" (just a few inches larger than the least-expensive thicker-plywood dollhouse "shells") to $250 for Greenleaf's huge ten-room "Garfield."

For slightly more money you can buy a dollhouse kit cut from a combination of ¼-inch and ⅜-inch plywood. These kits, available at larger craft and hobby stores and from dollhouse stores,

are made by Walmer Dollhouses, Houseworks ("Brittany" and "Heather"), Norm's Dollhouse ("Fairplay"), Real Good Toys (Simplicity series), Dee's Delights (Hometown series) and others. The interior and exterior walls and roofs are all precut with a saw, ready to nail and glue together. Most include windows (usually with printed mullions on the clear plastic glazing), doors, staircases and trim. Walmer has about six house kits, with ¼- and ⅜-inch plywood construction, that sell for $75 to $100. Prices for the basic two-story Colonial-style Simplicity, "Brittany," "Fairplay" and Hometown houses start at about $130 for a two-story six-room (including two rooms in the attic) house and range up to $300 for larger sizes. Finishing kits with clapboard and shingles for the smallest Walmer, Simplicity or

Fig. 1-13. Walmer's "Apple Blossom" has been customized with the company's clapboard siding, shingles,
an ornate porch railing, working windows and a new
front door.

Fig. 1-14. Walmer offers a two-story extension for
"Apple Blossom" to upgrade the dollhouse to eight
rooms.

Hometown houses run about $75. These simple Colonial-style houses are about 30 inches long, 24 inches high and 16 inches deep.

Prices go up as you select dollhouses with better quality construction. A similar-size two-story Colonial-style dollhouse kit is available in ⅜-inch-thick plywood from a number of firms for about $175. Dollhouse makers call these shells because they have no windows, doors, staircases, exterior siding or shingles but all the openings are cut. Some of the Walmer kits also feature milled slots in the interior walls (to accept the second-story interior floor) and interlocking interior floors for more rigid construction. These shells are usually designed to accept standard-size windows and doors from a number of firms, including Handley House, Houseworks, Alessio Miniatures, Norm's, Walmer and Timberbrook Wood Products. (See Fig. 1-11 and Fig. 1-12 on page 7.)

Windows and other finishing materials for the shells are plentiful, but you'll pay extra for them. Dozens of styles of windows and doors are available. The working windows cost $8 to $15 each, and doors are $10 to $20 each. Typically, a "starter" Colonial two-story dollhouse has five

windows, one exterior door and at least two interior doors, so the cost of doors and windows will be from $70 to $105. The materials to finish the exterior with clapboard, the chimney and foundation with brick or stone, shingles and trim will be another $100 to $200, depending on the complexity of the trim.

If you want a porch, plan on an additional $50 to $75. You can also add a wing to one or both sides of the house as a wing "shell" for $75 each. The extra door, window and exterior-finishing components for each shell will cost about $50. Or you can buy add-on extension wings that include the siding and windows for about $125 each.

Total cost for the average-size two-story Colonial-style dollhouse kit with a porch and a one-room addition, using the finest-quality materials and components, will be between $520 and $680. Those figures don't include finishing the interior walls, floors and ceilings, or adding working lights.

These are estimates, of course, for a typical unfurnished house. If you want a larger house, especially one of the Victorian, Colonial, Tudor or Southwestern-style kits, you might double or triple the cost. To spread out the expenses, start with the basic shell, and add components and finishing touches over many months. (See Fig. 1-13 and Fig. 1-14.)

SHOPPING FOR BARGAINS

The prices for the shells make the die-cut kits, made from ⅛-inch plywood, look like bargains. The die-cut dollhouses are, indeed, the kits that most people buy as their first project. Complete sets of working windows (to replace the non-working windows included in the kits) are available from Timberbook for about $130 for the Greenleaf "Garfield" and "Westville," $90 for the "Pierce" and $60 for the "Jefferson." So far, however, there are no other working windows available for any of the Greenleaf or Duracraft plywood kits. Many of the more complex porch or add-on room kits could be adapted to fit those kits.

It will take much longer to assemble the die-cut kits than to put together an equivalent saw-cut plywood kit. The die-cut parts must be carefully cut apart, sanded, fitted and sealed before assembly can begin. The windows and doors and their frames, when compared with the milled-wood factory-assembled accessory windows, are very time-consuming to prepare.

Chapter 3 discusses in detail the assembly of die-cut kits. I strongly suggest you read that chapter. Then, compare finished examples of the low-cost (⅛-inch-plywood) die-cut, mid-price (¼- and ⅜-inch-plywood) clapboard-surface and higher-cost (⅜-inch-plywood) bare-shell dollhouses before deciding that the less expensive kits are the bargains you are searching for.

FINDING MINIATURE LUMBERYARDS

Here's an astounding tidbit of information: There is probably a greater variety of windows, doors and shutters, milled-wood moldings and trim as well as a far broader array of laser-cut latticework trim for a 1/12-scale dollhouse than for a real house. In many cases, you also have a choice of woods. A complete selection of roofing materi-als as well as exterior brick, stone and wood siding is available. There is even a wide selection of hinges, doorknobs and porch lights. But finding these supplies can take some ingenuity, since many of the firms that make dollhouses and accessories are literally housed in private basements. Start looking locally, then expand your search to nearby cities and other parts of the country. You may even want to check in England, where the hobby is very active. Locating unusual items is part of the fun of the dollhouse hobby. Some suggestions on where to look follow.

You can buy dollhouse kits at many toy stores and craft shops. Accessory windows, trim and furnishings, however, are usually available only from stores that specialize in dollhouse minia-tures. Look in the yellow pages of your tele-phone book under "Dollhouses," "Hobby and Model Supplies—Retail" and "Miniature Items for Collectors" for sources. You may find some of what you need in each category. Not every store that carries dollhouse supplies has a listing under "Dollhouses." I have not found anything useful for l/12- or smaller-scale dollhouses at shops list-ed under any of the "Doll. . ." headings. Some of the "Miniatures" listings are for shops that sell miniature paintings and other tiny collect-ibles; some carry dollhouse furniture, accessories and supplies.

Other sources of information and supplies: Kalmbach Publishing sells a 400-page catalog of miniatures, and larger dollhouse dealers often have dozens of catalogs from which you can spe-cial order. There are also three dollhouse maga-zines that carry advertisements for dollhouse manufacturers and dealers. These publications have excellent stories and how-to articles in full color. *Nutshell News*, published monthly by Kalmbach, is the oldest and the most popular dollhouse magazine in America. *Dolls House World*, published bimonthly in England but widely distributed in America, is also an excel-lent publication. *Miniature Collector*, a bimonthly magazine published by Scott Publications, is another fine source of new ideas and products. Some dollhouse dealers and newsstands carry these magazines, or you can obtain sample copies from the publishers. See "Publications" in the back of this book.

SPACE FOR YOUR SECOND HOME

The smallest dollhouses are more than 2 feet long and 1 foot wide. Some of the ten-room Victorians are nearly 4 feet square. You will certainly need to plan for the space if you opt for one of the larger miniatures. Remember, too, that someday you may need to move the dollhouse out of the room. Most interior door openings are only 30 inches wide. If you are building a house that is, say, 48 inches wide by 48 inches deep, you may want to construct it in halves, using brackets and screws or door hinges with knockout pins as connecting links. You can then take the dollhouse apart to get it through the door. If you don't have a lot of space for the dollhouse and your main interest is in the miniature's exterior shape and style, consider building or buying one of the small-scale (half-scale or O-scale) houses without an interior.

THE DOLLHOUSE AS FURNITURE

Consider why you want a dollhouse. If what you really want is an array of rooms for decorating and displaying furniture, you may not wish to bother finishing the exterior of the miniature. One of the unfinished shells, either a kit or assembled, can be painted or stained and varnished on the exterior to look more like a piece of furniture than a model. And the dollhouse can be placed with its front permanently facing a wall.

Conversely, if you want to show the exterior of the dollhouse, perhaps with some of the landscaping shown in the color section and in Chapter 16, then you can place the open side of the dollhouse permanently against the wall.

If you want to see both the front and back of the dollhouse, it's most practical to place the house somewhere in the center of the room or with one end against the wall so it protrudes into the room like a peninsula. Or you can purchase a turntable.

Some dollhouse shops sell heavy-duty lazy-Susan-style turntables that you can place beneath the dollhouse. Even with this device, though, you will need a very wide shelf or table

with enough space for turning the dollhouse. The area must be somewhat larger than the longest diagonal dimension of the dollhouse.

A few shops carry special slide-out turntables, such as the Zero Clearance Turntable from The Quality Shoppe, that allow you to rest the dollhouse on a shelf or table against the wall, then slide the shelf out before you revolve it. The turntable must be mounted firmly on the shelf (and the shelf or table itself must be very heavy or anchored to the wall); otherwise, when the turntable is pulled out, the weight of the dollhouse may send everything crashing to the floor.

THE DOLLHOUSE AS A ROOM DIVIDER

Do you want the dollhouse to be on the floor or at a convenient viewing height? Bookcases placed back-to-back make excellent supports for a dollhouse and can be used to create a peninsula or room divider. At the center of the room display, a dollhouse is very attractive when stained and finished on three sides, so it has the appearance of a piece of furniture rather than a home-within-your-home.

INTERIOR DECORATING AND FURNISHINGS

You can apply any interior decorating technique to a 1/12-scale dollhouse. You name it, you can find it: wallpapers (many of them exact reprints of Victorian-era patterns), wood and vinyl floor coverings, rugs and carpets, wainscotings, railings and banisters, stairs and staircases as well as drapes and valances, corner trims, ceiling tiles and mirrors.

Imagine just about any lighting fixture—sconce, ceiling fan, chandelier or plain ceiling fixture—and you can probably find it in 1/12-scale. There are table and floor lamps in just about any style, too, and you can wire them to scale-sized light switches and outlet sockets on the walls. These lighting systems are exceptionally easy to install because they are connected by insulated copper tapes and the fixtures simply plug into the tapes.

This book is not intended to be an interior-decorating guide, but there are a few photos to give you an idea of the incredible array of products available and the intricate detail that's offered.

You can decorate the interior of your miniature home in virtually any style, from Victorian, Roaring Twenties and Art Deco to Colonial, Early American, modern and French or Italian Provincial. The furniture, drapes, wallpaper, paintings and frames and other accessories are available. There are even items like telephones, newspapers and magazines, groceries, silverware and fireplace tools. And you can find everything for a baby's nursery or a child's room.

Remember, you can do just about anything in a dollhouse that you can do in a real one. If you tire of the decor, go ahead and redecorate. It's certainly easier to repaint or to repaper the walls of a 12- x 15-inch room than a 12- x 15-foot room.

DECIDING ON A STYLE

You may find that with such a wide array of miniature furniture, you just can't decide which style you like best. One solution is to have two, three or more dollhouses. Some enthusiasts do just that. This gives them more rooms without having an excessively large dollhouse.

Other enthusiasts opt for two different houses with vastly different exterior and interior decor. Victorian-style dollhouses and furnishings are probably the most popular, followed closely by Colonial styles. Early American, rustic, Tudor, California bungalow, Art Deco, modern and Southwestern-style dollhouses and accessories are available, too. Remember, it's your home (or homes) within a home, so fulfill your dream.

CHAPTER TWO

STYLES AND SURFACE FINISHES

With a dollhouse, all your fantasies about creating and furnishing a dream home can become a reality. That reality may be only a twelfth the size of the house you occupy, but you still have virtually all the options you would have in designing a full-size home, including a choice of architectural style. Since the finish on the walls greatly influences the style of a house, in this chapter I'll describe the fundamental steps in finishing the exterior and suggest some specific dollhouses you can purchase (or customize) to capture the essence of each of the common architectural styles.

CLASSIC DOLLHOUSE STYLES

Is the dollhouse's exterior important to you? If you're interested only in what's inside, then use just an unfinished shell and insert windows to match the interior style. If you want to create an exterior as well, you can choose from every imaginable architectural style and decor. The classic, and most common, dollhouse style is usually referred to as Colonial, but it closely resembles American farmhouse. Several dollhouse kits are designed as Colonials, but most hobbyists redecorate farmhouses and transform them into true Colonials or Victorian-style houses.

A number of makers also offer dollhouse kits that effectively capture the essence of clapboard-siding-covered Cape Cods, frame-and-stucco Tudors, California bungalows, Southwestern-style adobe homes, raw-timber log cabins and even ultramodern homes and townhouses. You'll find furniture and interior decorating materials for all of these styles as well as Art Deco.

FARMHOUSES

The farmhouse design is simple, compact and relatively inexpensive to produce, making it one of the most common dollhouse styles. If you install windows only on the front wall, the way most dollhouse shells and the better kits are designed, the cost of adding working windows and doors is minimal. Most farmhouses have only four or five windows and a front door.

Some of the less expensive farmhouse-style kits come with built-in shutters, which can be sawed off for a simpler appearance. If you are adding working windows and doors, look for the numerous farmhouse styles.

Generally, farmhouse-style dollhouses are covered with clapboard wood siding. You could also cover the surface with simulated stone, capturing the style of a New England farmhouse, or with brick. In the color section, there's a photo of Dee's Delights' "Federal House," a bare shell decorated with Magic-Brik on the walls and Magic-Ston on the foundation. The shutters on the windows and the chimneys on both ends give it a Federal-style appearance. Remove the shutters, put a single chimney on the roof and add a porch, and it would look like a typical brick farmhouse.

Many real farmhouses were sheathed with

Fig. 2-1. The die-cut ⅛-inch plywood "Beacon Hill" is a classic Victorian mansion from Greenleaf. **Photo courtesy Greenleaf Products.**

Fig. 2-2. The interior of "Beacon Hill" includes stairs and a fireplace on every floor. **Photo courtesy Greenleaf Products.**

vertical 1 x 10 boards, and the seams between each board covered with 1 x 2 rounded-corner strips, to create what's called board-and-batten construction. You can simulate that construction on a bare plywood dollhouse shell by gluing on vertical ⅟₁₆ x ⅛-inch wood strips spaced ¾ inch apart. Use conventional wood angles for the trim at the corners.

VICTORIAN HOUSES

Dozens of dollhouse kits duplicate the ornate gabled roofs, towers and bay windows of Victorian-style houses. Some of the kits, such as Greenleaf Products' "Arthur" and Duracraft's "Lafayette," are simple one-story cottages with an attic. The lower-cost shells, such as Walmer Dollhouses' "Peaches and Cream," can be inexpensively decorated in Victorian style.

The grandeur of Victorian architecture is cap-

tured most effectively in the larger kits, such as "Woodstock" from Real Good Toys, shown in Chapter 4. These kits often have hinged front walls, making the houses deep enough to hold two rooms.

Greenleaf's spectacular "Garfield" or "Pierce," the medium-size "Beacon Hill" (see Fig. 2-1 and Fig. 2-2) and the more compact "Willowcrest" (see Fig. 2-3 on page 15) are examples of relatively inexpensive die-cut plywood houses. These ornate miniatures are extremely time-consuming projects, perhaps the most challenging of any dollhouses in this book.

It's relatively easy to add Victorian-style windows, fancy porches and a range of laser-cut wood trim to some of the better farmhouse-style kits and shells, which have standard-size window and door openings that will accept a wide choice styles. You'll also find stained-glass windows and kits to produce the lead-paned windows dis-

Fig. 2-3. The mansard-roofed "Willowcrest" from Greenleaf includes complex die-cut plywood ginger-bread trim. **Photo courtesy Greenleaf Products.**

Fig. 2-4. Fantasy Craft's "Tudor Cottage" kit includes windows, doors, chimney and trim. **Photo courtesy Fantasy Craft.**

cussed in Chapter 7. Part of the pleasure of finishing a plywood shell lies in the selection of just the "right" windows, doors and trim for your custom dollhouse.

Evergreen Woodworker's "Noel Thomas Tower House" or Norm's Dollhouse's "Seaside Villa" or "Georgetown" houses, shown in the color section of this book, are spectacular. The addition of laser-cut trim and ornate woodwork enhances the architectural design and proportions of these miniatures. The price of the unfinished shell, plus the cost of the exterior siding and brick surfaces, the working Victorian-style windows and the maze of trim, makes these houses about ten times more expensive to construct than die-cut Victorian houses of the same size.

There's almost no limit to the amount of money you can spend on decorating a Victorian dollhouse. Replicas of most complex milled wood trim shapes are available, sometimes in a

choice of woods, in 1/12-scale. There is also a selection of laser-cut-wood, cast-metal and etched-brass filigree trim for the peaks and eaves as well as weather vanes and fences. You'll even find real wood shingles. Also, examples of interior doors, woodwork trim, staircase railings, wainscoting, wallpaper, all types of hardwood floors, simulated crystal chandeliers and sconces, oriental rugs and furnishings abound in the Victorian style.

COLONIAL HOUSES

The classic farmhouse forms the basis for many of the relatively inexpensive Colonial-style dollhouses. Walmer offers the "Peaches and Cream" shell, shown in Chapter 1. With a different two-story gabled porch with four round columns, this version is called "Mint Julep," a classic Colonial. A similar basic farmhouse-style dollhouse, but with a shorter two-column porch, is available from Dee's Delights as the "Colonial" shell.

To give farmhouse shells a Colonial look, Houseworks, Walmer and others offer small dormers that fit most roofs. You can also create a simple Colonial style with an add-on, second-story covered porch and four columns cut from one-inch dowels.

Lawbre produces some beautiful Colonial-style dollhouse kits. Real Good Toys has

Fig. 2-5. Greenleaf's "Glencroft" is a Tudor-style four-room, die-cut, ⅛-inch plywood kit. **Photo courtesy Greenleaf Products.**

Fig. 2-6. The interior of "Glencroft" has a charming side staircase with a landing. **Photo courtesy Greenleaf Products.**

"Mulberry," with a two-story porch supported by four ornate columns, as well as the mansard-roofed "Monterey," with a solid back and removable front for access to the rooms. Greenleaf has the die-cut "Beaumont," a classic Southern-plantation-style house. Most larger dollhouse stores also offer Colonial-style shells, some made by local woodworkers.

TUDOR HOUSES

Several manufacturers offer Tudor-style dollhouses. Fantasy Craft has a simple four-room "Tudor Cottage," a shell kit cut from ⅜-inch birch hardwood. (See Fig. 2-4.) Greenleaf offers "Harrison," a die-cut, nine-room, Tudor-style house, as well as the smaller four-room "Glencroft." (See Fig. 2-5 and Fig. 2-6.) Some dollhouse stores also carry a few handmade shells and kits with Tudor-style roofs and bay windows.

With a few changes, simple one-story shells, such as Greenleaf's "Arthur," Duracraft's "Lafayette" and similar-style saw-cut plywood shells, such as Walmer's "Kiwi Cottage" and Real Good Toys' "Heather," also lend themselves nicely to Tudor decor. For example, the typical Tudor-style exterior wood framework can be simulated with ⅛ x ¼-inch-strips of wood that are stained, then cemented on the bare plywood walls. And the spaces between the strips can be

filled with one of the stucco paints described later in this chapter. For Tudor-style windows, Houseworks and other manufacturers make bay windows that you can modify. Simply form diamond-shaped panes from the wooden mullion strips included with the windows.

CALIFORNIA BUNGALOWS

Fantasy Craft makes a California bungalow, "Craftsman Bungalow," complete with a large dormer room on the second story. It has six rooms, a large front porch and an interesting array of windows. (See Fig. 2-7 and Fig. 2-8.) Some of the single-story dollhouse kits, including "Shady Grove" in Real Good Toys' Simplicity series, Houseworks' "Heather" and Walmer's "Kiwi Cottage," can be fitted with windows and trim to create the California bungalow appearance.

SOUTHWESTERN-STYLE HOUSES

Maureen O'Donnell offers two Southwestern-style simulated adobe dollhouse kits, one with a single room and an outside patio and the other with four rooms and an entryway patio. The kits are unusual in that they have no roof, just visible open beams that would support the missing ceiling. The construction is also unique. The walls are precut from Styrofoam insulation board. You

Fig. 2-7. This is Fantasy Craft's "Craftsman Bungalow."
Photo courtesy Fantasy Craft.

Fig. 2-8. The "Craftsman Bungalow" interior includes a
side staircase with a landing. Photo courtesy Fantasy
Craft.

Fig. 2-9. A Southwestern-style one-room adobe dollhouse shell with an enclosed patio is available as a kit
from Maureen O'Donnell.

Fig. 2-10. This one-story Southwestern-style dollhouse is
made from a ½-inch-thick Styrofoam shell produced by
Maureen O'Donnell.

Fig. 2-11. Access to the rooms in Maureen O'Donnell's
adobe house is through the open roof.

assemble the wall panels with carpenter's glue or
wall sizing, gently sand all the corners and edges
to a rounded profile, then cover the entire structure with wall-sizing compound. You add the
beams and windows last. (See Fig. 2-9, Fig. 2-10
and Fig. 2-11.)

Fantasy Craft produces two Southwestern-
style dollhouse kits, which must be assembled
from precut ½-inch-thick plywood, then sanded
and coated with sealer and mortar. The smaller
adobe-style "Pueblo House" has four rooms and

Fig. 2-12. "California Hacienda" is a 26 x 48-inch two-story Southwestern-style kit from Fantasy Craft. **Photo courtesy Fantasy Craft.**

Fig. 2-13. This is the interior of "California Hacienda." The spiral stairs are an AMSI product. **Photo courtesy Fantasy Craft.**

Fig. 2-14. Real Good Toys' "Adirondack Log Cabin" is a kit with a plywood shell and precut log finish.

an outdoor patio. The kit includes a flickering light to simulate wood burning inside a beehive-shaped stove.

The larger "California Hacienda" has seven rooms surrounding an enclosed two-story patio. You can add an impressive array of authentic details, including tile floors and steps, a tile roof, multi-pane doors and windows, Spanish-style chandeliers and wall sconces and simulated wrought-iron railings. (See Fig. 2-12 and Fig. 2-13.) Fantasy Craft offers complete packages of lights and wiring, exterior and interior finishing materials as well as door and window kits for all of these kits.

CONTEMPORARY AND ART DECO HOUSES

Though you'll find rooms full of contemporary and Art Deco furniture, very few dollhouses are available in such styles. Lolly's does produce some very modern dollhouses, including the two-story, eight-room "Citadel" with stained planking for the exterior walls and a curved staircase.

Of course, you can decorate any dollhouse with contemporary-style finishing materials. For instance, a peaked roof can be replaced with a flat one. And a steeply sloped roof on a larger dollhouse can be replaced with gently sloping panels so the house resembles a contemporary bungalow. Use a saw to cut the peaks on the sides of the house at the roof line to a shallower angle, and cut new ⅜-inch plywood roof panels because the gentler slope requires a longer roof. To further update the dollhouse, consider increasing the roof overhang by at least an inch on all sides. Remember, you will lose the space for any attic rooms. You may want to make the front and rear roof panels the same size, with no cutouts in the rear panel because access to the attic isn't needed.

LOG CABINS

Rustic-style dollhouses, with milled wood strips that represent squared-off rough-cut logs to cover the walls, are available as kits from several manufacturers. Real Good Toys makes two such models. "Blue Ridge Log Cabin" is a single-story house with two attic rooms; "Adirondack Log Cabin" is essentially the same house, but with a wide two-window dormer in the roof to make the upstairs rooms more useful. (See Fig. 2-14.) You finish the thin plywood shell by cutting the 26-inch-long rounded rectangular "logs" to length with a small coping saw. This same technique could be used to create a log cabin finish for virtually any single-story or farmhouse-style dollhouse kit.

Woodline Products offers an assembled log cabin made from dowels, giving both the exterior and the interior the look of real logs. The cabin has one room on the ground floor and a second in the attic. The building is nearly 2 feet square, including the full-width porch, so there is ample room for interior walls and furniture.

TOWNHOUSES

A typical townhouse has three or four rooms for an enthusiast to enjoy, but it takes up a minimum of shelf space. Real Good Toys makes the 38-inch-tall, three-story "Victorian Townhouse," a smaller replica of their Barbie™ doll-size Playscale™ house. In the Children's Choice series, the company also offers three smaller two- and two-and-a-half-story townhouses; each has a hinged front and solid rear wall. Walmer's three-story (plus attic) "Blueberry Pie Townhouse" has a hinged front wall.

Greenleaf makes a two-story (plus basement and attic) "Emerson Row" townhouse in their die-cut ⅛-inch plywood series. Norm's has a two-story San Francisco–style "Townhouse" shell designed to accept standard-size opening windows and doors (the other kits listed include nonopening windows). (See Fig. 2-15.) American Craft Products has a similar "Golden Gate View" kit with windows and doors. Also, many dollhouse stores carry townhouse shells produced by local woodworkers.

MINIATURE SHOPS, SCHOOLS AND CHURCHES

Ready to start a business or open a school? It's easy in miniature! You can create almost any building in an entire town, if you're so inclined. Plenty of possibilities exist for stores, schools and churches.

Fig. 2-15. Norm's "Townhouse" is sold as a plywood shell (right), either assembled or unassembled.

COUNTRY STORES

The counters, shelves, cash registers and many of the products you might find in a country grocery, toy store, music shop or hardware store come in l/12-scale, creating some interesting possibilities for furnishing a miniature retail business. Most of the single-story dollhouse kits lend themselves to simple conversions into country stores. Greenleaf outlines the steps for converting "Willowcrest" into a music store in *Dollhouses to Dream Houses*, Book III (Greenleaf). You'll have to cut a hole in one of the side walls to fit a large picture window, and you'll need a second hole in the same wall for a door. A 2 x 12-inch piece of ⅛-inch-thick wood, perhaps framed with some of the milled-wood moldings, can be used for a sign.

WESTERN-STYLE STORES

To create a store with the look of the Old West, add a ⅛-inch false front to the top portion of the side wall. The front should be the width of the side and extend from above the top of the door to about an inch above the peak of the roof. The roof pieces can be moved back so they still rest on the original roof and butt against the back of the false front. Paint the sign or false front, then use dry transfers (most stationary stores carry a variety of type sizes and faces) to letter a sign.

CITY-STYLE STORES

It's also easy to customize the first story of a townhouse into a ground-level urban store. You

Fig. 2-16. Fantasy Craft's "School House" has a removable roof for access to the interior. Photo courtesy Fantasy Craft.

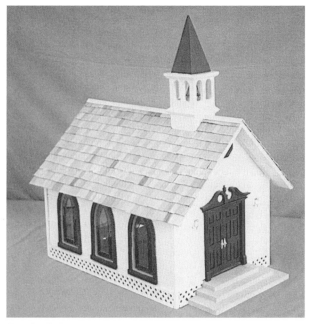

Fig. 2-17. An altar, pews, stained-glass windows and lighting are options with the Fantasy Craft "Church" kit. Photo courtesy Fantasy Craft.

can purchase large picture windows from a number of accessory suppliers, or cut and frame your own with the milled-wood window frames from Northeastern Scale Models.

Single-story "shadowbox" stores with removable tops and fixed backs are available from Real Good Toys (their "General Store"). The stores are also available from a number of woodworkers who sell through select dollhouse shops. American Craft Products makes a two-story store kit called the "Ol' Mercantile" with a removable back.

Pitty Pat Miniatures imports kits that replicate one- and two-story British stores, including the "Georgian," "High Street," "Regency," "Two-Story Regency" and "Two-Story York Street" shops.

The two-story stone-and-brick store shown in the color section started as a ⅜-inch plywood shell from Bill Lankford Creative Accents. The weathered appearance, created with light- and dark-gray stains, and the myriad details, such as trash and telephone wires, make this store an outstanding artistic creation. Bill Lankford describes his finishing techniques in classes at

dollhouse stores around the country. The real brick from "Handley House," applied as shown in Chapter 6, can be used to produce pleasing effects. (With practice, however, even vacuum-formed plastic brick panels can be painted to look as realistic as the bricks on these models.)

SCHOOLS AND CHURCHES

If you want to build a one-room school or church, Fantasy Craft offers ⅜-inch plywood shells and complete kits. Both structures have four walls with removable roofs. (See Fig. 2-16 and Fig. 2-17.) You can achieve similar results by converting many of the one-story dollhouse kits and shells into schools and churches. Real Good Toys' "Shady Grove" is one example, but most dollhouse dealers have similar one-story plywood shells available. To create a school, the door would have to be replaced with a window and a new door cut into one of the end walls.

To convert the house into a church, you might replace the windows (and door) with Houseworks' 12-pane 5024 windows with the half-round 5048 window tops and, perhaps, a

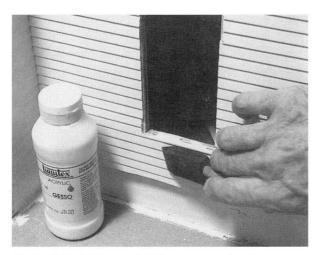

Fig. 2-18. Seal the wood with gesso, wood sealer or sanding sealer.

Fig. 2-19. Use a brush the width of the clapboards to make it easier to apply the final coats of paint.

matching 6016 double-entry door fitted into one end of the shell. You'll need to enlarge the existing window and door openings with an electric saber saw or a handheld coping saw. A pair of chimneys could serve as a simulated steeple, or you could fabricate a more complex one from wood. Betty's Wooden Miniatures makes a ventilated steeple that would work for either the church or the school.

PAINT, STUCCO AND OTHER FINISHES

Exterior finish determines so much of a dollhouse's look that you may want to consider finish options at the same time you select the kit. For example, you may decide to forgo a typical exterior, such as clapboard, and opt instead for a stained and varnished shell so the model's finish blends with that of your furniture. Perhaps you'll want a plain shell (no surface coverings) so you can finish the walls in stucco or simulated board-and-batten wood.

To get an idea of how crucial the finish is to a dollhouse's style, consider some of the unique facades of the newest full-size townhouses. A photo of these is shown in the color section, illustrating the vast difference a change in exterior surface makes in what is really a row of identical townhouses. Using an array of dollhouse

products, you can duplicate just about any of these surface finish styles.

EXTERIOR PAINT

The proper time to paint the exterior of a dollhouse is after the finish is complete but before the trim, windows or doors are installed. It's a good idea to seal the entire surface, both inside and out, of a ⅜- or ½-inch plywood dollhouse with gesso or sanding sealer. (See Fig. 2-18.) Seal all the parts of a die-cut 1/8-inch dollhouse with a mixture of lacquer-based shellac or Deft Clear Wood Finish and thinner. (Be sure to work outdoors or in a well-ventilated area.)

When the surface dries, check for splinters on exposed edges that will not be covered by trim or windows, and sand the rough edges smooth. Now you're ready to paint. You can use any of the interior latex wall paints intended for real houses, but for the trim, you may want a smaller quantity or a color that's not available from a conventional paint store.

The following latex paints, made specially for dollhouses, come in 8-ounce jars: Builder's Choice Paints, from New England Hobby Supply, has nearly 100 colors and stains. Deco Art Americana latex paint, from Dee's Delights, comes in about 60 colors. Borden's Accent paints are also available in small containers from some hardware stores.

Whichever paint you choose, apply it with a 1-inch-wide brush or a disposable sponge brush. (See Fig. 2-19). Carefully fit all of the trim, then paint each piece separately before gluing it in place as described in Chapter 8. The techniques for painting windows and doors are described in Chapter 7.

STUCCO

Stucco is an easy surface to duplicate. Simply add one of the granular antiskid deck compounds, which are intended for full-size boat decks or patios, to interior latex house paint in your choice of color. (Be sure to test a small amount of compound and paint to be sure you'll achieve the texture and color you desire.) Then apply, in a single step, both the color and surface texture to the dollhouse.

Dee's Delights' "Magic Stucco" or Greenleaf's "Dollhouse Stucco" also produces the appearance of stucco. First, seal the surface of the dollhouse as described above and let it dry. Then, apply the stucco compound with a 1-inch sponge brush. After it dries, apply a final coat of paint.

Many of the dollhouse kits include clapboard wood siding. You can also buy easy-to-fit milled-wood panels and install them as described in the sections on clapboard sheathing in Chapter 5. Or you can purchase vacuum-formed plastic panels that simulate clapboard.

For a brick exterior, use the real miniature brick, apply vacuum-formed plastic panels that simulate brick, or try the clever Magic-Brik system from Dee's Delights (shown in the color section). The techniques for installing all of these types of brick are described in Chapter 6.

Several styles of cut stone are duplicated in a wide assortment of vacuum-formed plastic panels. Lawbre makes individual stones and 4 x 4-inch panels that simulate rectangular cut stones, square-cut stones (for walls, foundations or chimneys) and slates (for floors or sidewalks). Magic-Ston, from Dee's Delights, is another option; it's applied just like Magic-Brik. There's a photo of a chimney being finished with both materials in the color section. Similar products from Dee's Delights allow you to duplicate concrete blocks with Magic-Bloc or slate with Magic-Slat.

RIVER ROCK AND FIELDSTONE

To create the appearance of river rock on a foundation, chimney or complete wall, buy some pre-sorted ¼-inch gravel from a garden supply or construction outlet. Lawbre makes a similar-shaped plastic stone called Fieldstones, which can be stained, then installed.

To apply the stone, lay the dollhouse on its side so the wall you are decorating is horizontal. Cover the surface with about ⅛ inch of tile grouting (made for use in a full-size house) or Miniature House's Mortar Gray or Mortar White compound. Push the rocks in place while the material is still wet. Let the wall dry overnight, then repeat the process on the remaining walls.

This Victorian mansion started as a bare plywood "Seaside Villa" shell from Norm's Dollhouse. David Nielsen finished the exterior and interior.

David Nielsen finished the exterior and interior of this mansion starting with the "Georgetown" plywood shell from Norm's Dollhouse.

The "Noel Thomas Tower House," by Evergreen Woodworker, is available as a bare plywood shell. Norm Nielsen finished the exquisite exterior with Northeastern Scale Models siding and laser-cut wood trim.

These four full-size townhouses are the same building, but notice how windows and exterior finish change their appearance.

CHAPTER THREE

DIE-CUT DOLLHOUSE KITS

If you choose a dollhouse kit from Greenleaf Products or Duracraft, you have lots of company. These are the most popular models ever manufactured; they are also the least expensive kits by a wide margin. Their distinctive feature is that virtually every part is made from ⅛-inch die-cut plywood. (See Fig. 3-1 and Fig. 3-2.)

LEARNING FROM INSTRUCTIONS

When you open one of these dollhouse kits, all you see is a stack of ⅛-inch plywood sheets. Look carefully, though, and you'll notice that each sheet has been precut in the shapes of walls, windows, trim and hundreds of unidentifi-

Fig. 3-1. Greenleaf's "Arthur" is one of the least expensive complete dollhouse kits. **Photo courtesy Greenleaf Products.**

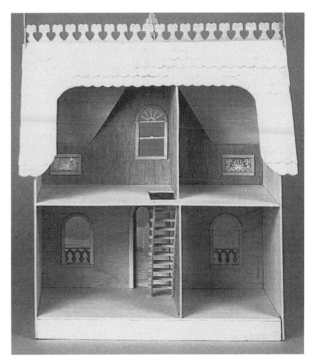

Fig. 3-2. The "Arthur" interior includes stairs and window frames. The kit also comes with trim and individual shingles. **Photo courtesy Greenleaf Products.**

able pieces. It might seem that the assembly will be as easy as putting together a cardboard toy: Just punch out the parts, fit the tabs into their slots, apply glue, and paint. Voilà!—you have the dollhouse pictured on the box lid. Well, it's actually a bit more complicated than that.

Think of these kits as the ultimate in puzzles, and you'll have the right mind-set. All the cleverly designed parts fit together and each part has its place, but unlike colored puzzle pieces, these are identifiable only by their shape.

Read the instructions carefully. It seems that most of us kit-builders have an attitude problem: We somehow feel that just because we picked out the kit, we're smarter than the instruction writers think we are. Wrong. I've been building kits of all kinds for nearly 50 years. I enjoy doing this sort of thing for a living, and I could not properly assemble any of these dollhouse kits without reading the instructions. How do I know this? Guess. There's a good chance you cannot correctly assemble one without reading (and understanding) the instructions, either.

You'll find that all the parts really are there. What's more, the assembly sequence is pretty logical. The die-cutting process allows the manufacturer to make some truly complex dollhouses at a relatively low cost. In fact, you would spend about $2,000 to duplicate a $200 Greenleaf with a conventional ⅜-inch plywood dollhouse. In terms of size and style per dollar, these kits are incredible bargains.

IS THIS KIT FOR YOU?

With die-cut dollhouse kits, what you save in money you'll probably spend in time. The same process that makes these kits so easy to manufacture makes them more time-consuming for you to assemble. No part is thicker than ⅛ inch. That means that the ⅜- or ½-inch-thick doors and windows in the more expensive kits must be built up from three or four layers of die-cut plywood.

It is much easier to install windows and doors in the more expensive kits. The less expensive ⅜-inch plywood dollhouses often have windows that need to be assembled from five pieces of wood (the more expensive kits have one-piece

preassembled windows). Each piece is cut precisely to size, however, and no sanding is necessary other than to remove excess fuzz that's visible after the first coat of paint sealer. The parts almost fall into their precut openings.

Each of the four or five pieces that make up the layers of each window a die-cut kit must be carefully sliced from the sheet with a hobby knife, sanded, and painted with sealer. Then they must be sanded again and carefully aligned during assembly. This time-consuming process can be frustrating if you really want is a finished dollhouse, rather than the "joy" of building.

Lots of folks do enjoy building die-cut plywood kits. Some have built dozens for stores, for friends or for gifts. Others spend hundreds of hours customizing an inexpensive kit, putting time, rather than money, toward the goal of creating a pleasing miniature house. You'll know whether these kits are suitable for you within a few hours of opening the box. Do give the die-cut a chance, though, before you opt to start over with one of the more expensive saw-cut ⅜-inch plywood kits. Then, if you find you've worked for a dozen hours or more and have seemingly accomplished nothing, give up. Admit that what you really want is a "fall-together" kit, and go out and buy one of the finished plywood shells or simple kits with windows. Most of these can be assembled, painted and finished in less time than it takes to cut out and prepare the parts for a similar-size die-cut kit. So swallow hard and throw money at the problem.

CARPENTER'S TOOLS

You'll need more than your fingers and glue to assemble any of the die-cut plywood dollhouse kits. I'd recommend an X-Acto number 1 hobby knife with two or three packages of number 2 blades. A new blade is the only labor-saving device you can buy to ease the assembly of these kits. The blades dull quickly cutting through glue-soaked plywood so I'd suggest checking the blade every hour or so. If it's chipped, dull or nicked, replace it. Figure that the smallest of these dollhouses will consume about a dozen blades. Use a steel ruler to guide the blade along any partially missing seams.

Fig. 3-3. Cut completely through each corner with a hobby knife.

Fig. 3-4. Turn the wall 90 degrees and cut through the corner from the new direction.

Buy a sanding tool complete with 220 grit sandpaper, then purchase another half dozen sheets. Scrounge up a piece of 1 x 3 hardwood to use as a block for sanding square corners, and borrow a short tool handle to use as a sanding block for rounded inside corners.

Few nails or screws are needed for the tab-in-slot assembly system, but you will use a lot of glue. Common white glue is strong enough to hold these interlocked parts in place and has the advantage of drying clear, should you want to stain some part. I prefer the slightly yellow carpenter's glue because it is less likely to crack under extreme temperature changes. Pick up some refillable syringes to apply controlled beads of glue.

Hot glue, applied with a glue gun, is not a wise choice for these dollhouses. Because it's difficult to apply hot glue in small amounts, fillets may build up in inside corners and will be difficult to cover with wallpaper or paneling. If you're skilled at using a hot glue gun, however, you may find it works well for filling in the outside corner seams around the interlocking tabs.

CUTTING OUT THE PARTS

Before you try to remove any part, read the instructions. Look at the parts while they are still in their plywood sheets to be sure you can identify every piece. For example, you want to be certain that a little tab belongs to the wall, and not to some adjacent basement edge. The goal here is to be 100 percent sure which part is important and which is scrap wood.

The term "die-cut" is somewhat misleading; if the kits were completely cut, you'd have a box full of pieces, not a box full of plywood sheets. Small wisps of wood hold the parts together where the steel dies did not penetrate completely around the edges of the parts—usually the corners.

To cut the pieces apart, lay the a plywood sheet on a sturdy working surface covered with a single sheet of corrugated cardboard or a self-healing cutting mat available at large art-supply stores. Cut firmly into one angle of each corner with the X-Acto number 1 knife and number 2 blade. (See Fig. 3-3.) Wiggle the blade to push its

Fig. 3-5. Use both thumbs to wiggle the windows out. Save the pieces to use as shutters.

Fig. 3-6. Wrap sandpaper around a 1 x 3 to make a sanding block.

tip right through the wood. Turn the knife 90 degrees and slice into the corner from the other direction. (See Fig. 3-4.) Repeat the process with all of the corners.

Use both thumbs to wiggle the part from the sheet of plywood. (See Fig. 3-5.) Watch carefully for areas that catch because they're not cut clear through. If you find such a spot, put the part back on the cutting board and slice through the attached area.

You'll find numerous splinters hanging from the edges of some of the parts, and here's where the sanding begins. Always use some kind of sanding block at this point; bare sandpaper will round the edges and corners. Use a sanding block tool with a roll of *220* grit sandpaper.

To sand window openings and inside frames, hold the sandpaper firmly on a 1 x 3-inch wood sanding block so the sanded edges and corners will be crisp and square. (See Fig. 3-6.) Do the same for inside corners. Use the round handle to support the sandpaper when sanding rounded, inside corners. (See Fig. 3-7 and Fig. 3-8.) The block is good for smoothing flat surfaces.

ASSEMBLING TAB-IN-SLOT PIECES

Once you've identified every part, you know how all the pieces will fit together. This is the time to do a test run. Using masking tape to hold the parts in their slots, install the walls, floors, foundation and roof. (See Fig. 3-9.) Build a complete dollhouse "shell" from those die-cut (and now, free at last) ⅛-inch plywood parts. You'll find that the house would very nearly stand without the masking tape, thanks to all those slots and tabs that hold and align the major parts.

If you intend to make modifications to the kit, do so before you assemble any of the parts. For instance, if you want to replace any or all of the doors and windows with milled-wood components, test-fit those parts now to be sure the openings do not need to be enlarged. If you're going to put in a more detailed staircase, check it for fit. Decide if you want to move any of the internal walls or add more walls. When you are satisfied, paint all the parts with an equal mixture of lacquer-based shellac or Deft Clear Wood and thinner to seal the surfaces and edges. If you

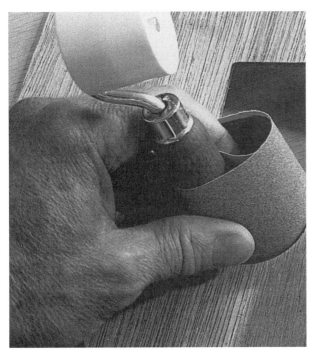

Fig. 3-7. Wrap sandpaper around a handle to sand inside curved windows.

Fig. 3-8. Use a sanding block to smooth the flat surfaces.

are going to use stucco or board-and-batten for the exterior, be sure to fill all the visible corner seams and interlocking tabs with putty. (See Fig. 3-10.) Sand the filled-in corners smooth with the sanding block.

If all is well, disassemble the parts and follow the assembly sequence shown in the instructions. Use the glue syringe to run an even bead of glue along the joining edge of each part and press the piece into place. It's wise to assemble a floor and two adjoining walls first. Use a carpenter's try square or some old books to be certain that this first corner is perfectly square, and let its glue joints dry overnight. Repeat the process with each major corner, but be sure you've added any interlocking floors or interior walls before you allow the glued joints to dry. Take your time, allowing several nights for this basic assembly.

THE DIE-CUT SHELL

You now have what the dollhouse stores call a shell. The shell provides a strong surface for the

addition of exterior clapboard, brick, stone or shingle wall. From here, you can finish the die-cut dollhouse with the suggestions in the kit (some include clapboard siding or shingles), or you can opt for any of the exterior finishes available for the more expensive shells.

Greenleaf suggests that you install their windows, then apply the exterior surfaces so they abut the outer edges of all the windows, door frames and trim. That's not the way it's done on a real house, but you can get away with it if you use the Greenleaf clapboards or thin vacuum-formed plastic brick or stone exterior surface panels from Holgate and Reynolds, JR Enterprises or Precision. These materials are thin enough so the die-cut plywood window frames are about flush with the final exterior wall surface. There's a photo in the color section of a Greenleaf half-scale "Fairfield" completely covered with vacuum-formed plastic clapboard, brick, stone and shingle panels from Precision.

The easiest way to finish the exterior of a Greenleaf or Duracraft dollhouse is simply to paint it with Greenleaf Dollhouse Stucco or Dee's Delights Magic-Stucco, or to apply

Fig. 3-9. Test-fit all the major panels in their grooves and slots.

Fig. 3-10. Use putty to fill in around the assembled grooves and slots so they won't be as obvious as these on the finished dollhouse.

vertical ¹⁄₁₆ x ⅛-inch strips of wood every ¾ inches to simulate board-and-batten wood walls. With these methods, the window frames can be painted and installed after the walls are finished, so you can be a bit less careful when painting the walls.

The dollhouse will look more realistic, however, if you first install prepainted window and door frames. The wall paint (and the glue that holds the window and door frames) will build up a gusset that makes the frames look like they are part of the walls rather than resting on top of them. You'll just have to be more careful when painting the stucco or board-and-batten so you don't smear the window and door frames.

The Tudor-style stained-wood framework looks especially toylike if it is applied on top of paint. For more realism, stain or paint the trim as well as all the door and window frames, and glue them in place. Finish the surface of the walls by brushing on Greenleaf's Dollhouse Stucco or Dee's Delight's Magic-Stucco so it flows right up against the base of the trim and frames. This technique makes it look as though the trim and frames are buried in a plaster exterior.

INSTALLING WINDOWS AND DOORS

I would suggest you install the windows and frames and trim after the walls are completely assembled, regardless of the sequence you select for painting walls, windows and doors. It's a bit more awkward than working with the unassembled flat panel walls, but it is far easier to be certain the frames are perfectly square.

Sand each window, door and frame thoroughly. Paint the windows and doors with at least three coats of sanding sealer, wall sizing or gesso. Between each coat, use a sanding block and 220 sandpaper to sand away any fuzz. The grain of every one of these die-cut window and door frames will run up and down, rather than across, so those horizontal areas must be sanded and sealed with particular care.

If you want these components to look like the milled-wood parts in more expensive kits, you'll have to apply at least three coats of filler, sanding with the sanding block after each coat dries. Take your time preparing the parts. Paint the windows, frames and trim, and lay them on waxed paper to dry.

I'd suggest placing the house on the floor when you install the outer window frames, and work on one wall at a time. Apply white glue to the back of each window and door frame, and center it as perfectly as you can around each opening. Stand back and take a good look at the wall from several angles. All frames should be aligned with one another and the foundation should align with the vertical walls. Let each wall dry overnight before progressing to the next wall.

Finish the interior with lights, stairs and fireplaces, flooring and wall coverings, as described in Chapters 11, 12, 13 and 14, before adding the inner window frames, clear plastic glazing and mullions. The quick-stick cements (like Tacky Glue and Quick Grab) work well for installing these parts. Put a small bead of cement onto the part, press it in place and align it. Work with the dollhouse turned on its side so you can get a better look at the inside to be certain the interior frames are perfectly aligned with the ceiling, floor and walls.

If you run out of patience sanding, painting and aligning die-cut windows and doors, consider replacing them with milled-wood parts. If you have a Greenleaf "Westville," "Jefferson," "Garfield" or "Pierce" dollhouse, you can buy a complete set of ready-made milled-wood working windows and doors from Timberbrook. (The windows in most of the other Greenleaf and Duracraft dollhouses are replicas of designs and shapes that are not readily available as accessory windows.) Replacing the windows, though, requires some major cutting and fitting: You will have to use an electric saber saw or a handheld jig saw to enlarge every die-cut opening to fit the nearest-size ready-made window or door.

The more expensive dollhouse kits and shells have walls made of ⅜-inch plywood, which is usually covered with another ⅛ inch of milled-wood clapboard or Houseworks real bricks. In

1/12-scale, the resulting ½-inch-thick wall is 6 inches thick, just like a real house. The milled-wood replacement windows and doors are designed for walls that are at least ⅜ inches thick, and most working windows are meant to fit into walls that are ½ inch thick.

The ⅛-inch-thick die-cut plywood wall is only 2 inches thick in l/12-scale. If you use the layered windows from the kit, the thickness won't be a problem. Timberbrook provides special thin frames in the sets for the Greenleaf "Westville," Jefferson," "Garfield" and "Harrison." But if you want to use the milled-wood windows from Houseworks, Handley, Timberbrook, Alessio and others, you will need to add spacers so the windows do not protrude a full ¼ inch into the interior. There are two possibilities: One is to cover the outside of the dollhouse with a ⅛-inch-thick layer of Northeastern or similar milled clapboard siding, or with a layer of Houseworks 8201 real-brick Common Bricks or the similar Houseworks 8206 and 8207 styrene plastic bricks, described in Chapter 6. The other possibility is to add an inner frame of ⅛-inch-square wood around each window and door to space them out from the walls, and leave the frames flush with the inside wall surfaces.

ADDING THE FINAL TOUCHES

Once you have determined how to finish the exterior walls and installed the windows, doors and trim of your choice, the construction of a die-cut kit varies little from that of any other dollhouse kit. Chapters 8, 9 and 10 describe the methods for installing trim, porches, chimneys and roofs. The interior work is virtually identical for ⅛-inch die-cut plywood and ⅜-inch saw-cut plywood dollhouses. The inexpensive die-cut dollhouses lend themselves nicely to finished exterior landscaping, too. There are photographs, in the color section, of Greenleaf's "Arthur" and Duracraft's "Lafayette," which can be readily customized.

Greenleaf publishes three booklets, *Dollhouses to Dreamhouses*, Volumes I, II and III, which illustrate methods for upgrading and detailing their die-cut dollhouses.

CHAPTER FOUR

CUSTOM DOLLHOUSE SHELLS AND KITS

The better-quality dollhouses, which are saw-cut from plywood, are exact-scale replicas of real houses in virtually every respect, right down to the doorknobs. This ensures that the furnishings, which are also 1/12-scale, will be in precise proportion to the rooms and the whole house. From the working wall switches to the exterior bricks, the dollhouse will look right and realistic.

SAW-CUT REALISM

The saw-cut dollhouses use ⅜-inch plywood for the exterior walls and, in some cases, ¼-inch plywood for interior walls and floors. The ⅜-inch plywood is usually covered with another ⅛ inch of exterior clapboard, bricks or other texture. The resulting exterior wall is a half-inch thick—in 1/12-scale, that's 6 inches, about the thickness of a wall in a real house.

Accessory doors and windows, and those furnished with complete kits or accessory packs, have frames designed to fit into ⅜- and ½-inch-thick walls—again, the same thickness as the real thing. The windows and doors themselves are, of course, made from milled wood that is exactly 1/12-scale, with doorknobs, hinges, window pulls, window locks and catches all available. The knobs, locks and catches do not, however, actually operate.

The lower-cost nonworking windows and the built-up windows assembled from finished pre-cut milled-wood frames are designed for ⅜-inch-thick walls. The working windows and the more ornate doors are designed to fit into ½-inch-thick walls. Chapter 7 describes how to install windows and compensate for differences in the depth of the frames compared with the thickness of the walls.

BUILDING A DOLLHOUSE

Dollhouse enthusiasts call the basic shape of the dollhouse the shell, which is the first part of the dollhouse that must be finished. The shell can be compared to the framework or studs of a real house, with the interior surfaces covered with plaster board (or lath-and-plaster, if your imagination insists on that kind of quality) and the exterior covered with insulation board ready for the final exterior finish. A few of the lower-cost kits include ⅜-inch-plywood outer walls that have grooves milled into the surface to represent clapboard for an automatic exterior.

The chapters of this book are arranged to provide a logical progression in finishing most kits. The experience of hundreds of dollhouse builders suggests that this is a sensible sequence. The die-cut ⅛-inch plywood dollhouses sometimes require a change in the steps, and that's described in Chapter 3.

Dollhouses deviate somewhat from the sequences used in completing a real house, but those differences make construction easy and enjoyable. It's actually fun to paint miniature windows and trim as separate pieces, rather than struggling to paint them after they are in place.

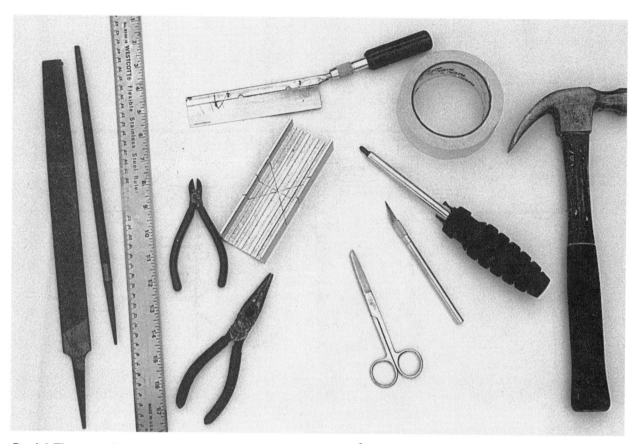

Fig. 4-1. These are the basic tools needed to assemble and finish a ⅜-inch plywood dollhouse kit.

I strongly advise finishing the exterior before tackling the inside because windows and doors and their frames must be fitted in place before you can finish the interior walls. Follow the finishing sequence chapter by chapter, starting with porches and fireplaces and progressing through wiring, wall and ceiling finishing, floor coverings and interior trim.

PLANNING AHEAD

How do you envision your finished dollhouse? If you want a front or side porch, decide now, because you may want to add a door or window to reach the porch. Do you want additional rooms (the dollhouse manufacturers often refer to them as extensions or wings) on the right or left side of the house? If so, you'll need to cut doors for them in the adjoining exterior walls. If you want side doors or windows, this is the time to cut the holes for these fittings.

Plan the interior now, too. If you are going to replace the stairs, buy new ones and assemble them at least to the stage where you can temporarily fit them in place. You may need to enlarge the holes in the floors or cut new holes. If you want fireplaces, you may want to build or buy exterior chimneys to match their locations. Similarly, this is the time to decide if you want any exterior lighting, so you can put the wiring in place and locate the fixtures before applying the exterior finish.

You can usually move most of the interior walls after the exterior is finished. You can, in fact, leave some of the walls loose until it's time to wire the interior and finish the walls, ceilings and floors.

CARPENTER'S TOOLS

All parts in the better dollhouse kits are cut for you, including any exterior siding. These kits are a joy to assemble because everything fits so nicely and all the wood, including the knot-free plywood, is of excellent quality. You will, however, need to do some minor cutting and fitting if you intend to finish the interior, especially if you want to add baseboards and other trim.

The tools needed to assemble a quality dollhouse kit include a ruler, pencil, hammer, needlenose pliers, flat file and masking tape. (See Fig. 4-1.) You will want to prepunch most nail holes, but you can use the needlenose pliers to hold one of the nails, or you can buy a thin-bladed awl just for that purpose. Use the flat file to square off corners of the window and door openings. Some kits use screws for assembly, particularly on hinged front wall panels, so you may need a screwdriver as well.

Replacement windows and doors are designed to fit in standard-size openings. If you intend to change those parts, check with your dealer to be sure the new ones will work in your dollhouse kit. If not, find out if windows or doors are available to fit the existing openings. Fortunately, it's not that difficult to enlarge the window or door openings using an electric saber saw or even a handheld jig saw.

To cut and fit wood interior trim as well as more ornate milled or laser-cut wood for the exterior, you'll need a hobbyist's miter box and a razor saw. Use a hobby knife, such as an X-Acto number 1 knife with number 2 blades, and scissors to cut wallpaper and paper patterns to finish interior floors. You'll need diagonal cutters to install wiring inside the house. Needlenose pliers come in handy when you're working with wiring, and they can be useful in preparing bricks and other exterior details.

Use waxed paper to keep freshly painted windows from sticking to your workbench while they dry. And cover your workbench with waxed paper when gluing windows or other parts together, so they won't stick to the work surface if any glue oozes out of the joints.

GLUES AND CEMENTS

Common white glue or carpenter's glue is best for assembling shells and window or door kits. You can use hot glue, but it's difficult to glue a joint without leaving a fillet that might interfere

with adding exterior trim or show through wallpaper. A glue syringe, like a Monojet, is handy for applying white or carpenter's glue. Store the syringe in an empty jar or can filled with an inch or so of water. The water will keep the glue in the tip of the syringe from solidifying.

Specific dollhouse finishes sometimes require special glues. I would strongly recommend Quick Grab Cement by 3C for installing any milled-wood clapboard siding. Applying wallpaper requires special paste; try Mini Graphics' Wallpaper Mucilage because it dries slower than most wallpaper pastes. To glue metal or plastic to wood, use clear silicone bathtub caulking.

PREPARING THE PARTS

Most saw-cut panels require little or no sanding until after you've applied the first coat of sanding sealer. Then, you should sand small splinters and wisps of wood flat.

The saws that manufacturers use to cut most of the window and door openings leave a small radius in each corner. File all four corners of each opening square with a flat or square file. Test-fit the windows and doors to be sure you've removed enough material so they fit, with about $\frac{1}{64}$ inch of movement. That extra space will be taken up later with paint.

The top-grade plywood of the better kits and shells doesn't need a sealer, but I still recommend that you paint both the inside and outside of every surface with an acrylic wood sealer. A sealer will make the cement that holds an exterior finish material (such as clapboard) easier to use, and it will ensure that the wiring tape for interior wiring will stick to the walls. I find it easier to paint the dollhouse after it's assembled, but you may choose to paint the pieces before assembly.

If you have decided to stain the exterior or interior of the dollhouse so it looks like a piece of furniture, apply the stain to all the parts before assembling them. The cement and glues will affect how well the stain covers the wood, and they will show as spots and lighter areas on the finished project. When the stain is dry, paint all the surfaces with a clear sealing compound such as Deft Clear. If you later decide that you'd rather have the dollhouse look like a miniature

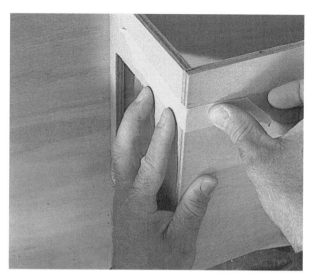

Fig. 4-2. Use 1-inch-wide masking tape to hold the parts in place while nailing and until the glue dries.

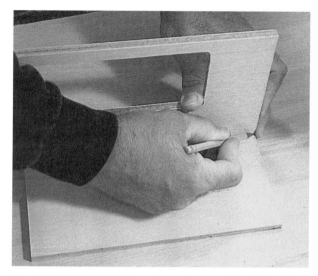

Fig. 4-3. Mark the inside edges of any walls in "blind" corners.

house, you can cover the exterior with paint, clapboard, brick or any other finish.

PUTTING THE PIECES TOGETHER

Do read every word of the kit's instructions. If some of the suggestions for assembly techniques or sequences differ from mine, decide which will work best for you. Identify all the parts, and lay them out in an exploded form or temporarily tape them together so you are certain where each part fits.

FITTING, CLAMPING AND NAILING

Each joint should be both glued and nailed, even on dollhouses with interior walls slotted to hold the floors. If you are used to working with woodworkers' clamps, use them to hold the pieces together. Masking tape works just as well, however, if you do it right.

Buy the best 1-inch-wide masking tape you can find. Place the tape on the panel that will be joined on its plywood face. Pull the tape over the end with the visible layers of wood and down over the second piece. The sequence is shown, step-by-step, in photographs for installing the roof. (See "Clamping the Roof" on pages 36 and 37.) Put a piece of tape every 9 inches or so

along the seam. Adjust the fit of the two pieces, held by clamps or masking tape, until it is perfect. (See Fig. 4-2.)

If you are inexperienced at carpentry, use the following technique to avoid splitting the wood as you drive in the nails: First, prepunch the nail holes. To do so, mark the position of the nails with a pencil. Remove the clamps or tape. Hold one of the nails in needlenose pliers while you tap the nail gently into the wood (or you can use a thin-bladed awl to make the hole). Then, pound the nail through the wood. Temporarily hold the adjoining piece in place to be sure the nail is going down the center of the end of the second piece of plywood. If the nail is offset, use a second nail, driven at the correct angle, and recheck its entry.

Run a thick bead of glue along the edge of the part with the visible wood plies. This will give the glue the best chance to sink into the grain.

Reassemble the two parts with the clamps or masking tape precisely as before. The nails can then be driven flush with gentle taps from a standard-size hammer. Keep a wet rag handy to wipe away all traces of glue that ooze from the joint.

ASSEMBLING WALL-TO-WALL JOINTS

If a joint between two pieces is not at a corner, some additional steps will be needed. These T-

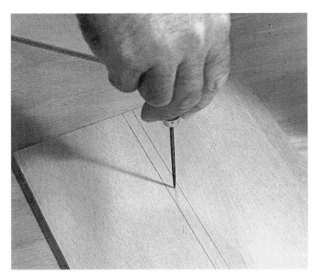

Fig. 4-4. Use an awl or nail to prepunch all the nail holes through the plywood.

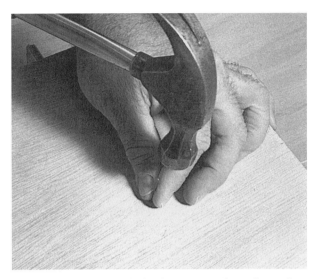

Fig. 4-5. Tap lightly with the hammer to drive the nail into the edge of the adjoining wall.

shaped joints are common in larger dollhouses and at all the roof-to-wall joints.

Temporarily assemble the parts. If there is any chance the panels could move while you mark them, hold them tightly together with masking tape or clamps. Use a pencil to mark the locations of both the right and left sides of the joint. (See Fig. 4-3.) Also mark small arrows, on the joining side of the panel, to indicate where you want to drive nails.

Remove the panels. Drive a nail or awl, centered directly between the two lines, through the wall. Remove the nail. Drive three or four nails along the joining face and remove them. (See Fig. 4-4.) Turn the joining panel over and reassemble the two parts with a bead of glue, using the pencil lines to be sure the panels are back together in precisely the same location. Drive nails, now on the opposite side of the wall, through each of the holes you just made. (See Fig. 4-5.) The nails should go right into the center of the adjoining wall so there is no chance of splitting the wood.

INSTALLING HINGED FRONT WALLS

Some of the larger townhouse-style kits have hinged front walls. The two-story wall panel beneath the diamond-shaped window on Real Good Toys' "Woodstock" house, shown at the end of this chapter, is a hinged wall. Hinged

walls add nothing to the strength of the finished dollhouse, but to be certain they will work, the walls must be fitted before you make the first glue-and-nail joint.

When you are test-fitting parts that are held together only by masking tape, be sure to put hinged walls in their correct position. Test-fit the hinged wall when the actual glue-and-nail assembly process reaches the panels that will be adjacent to it. The hinged wall itself should not be installed until all the glue joints have had a few days to dry.

Most kits do not include instructions on how to recess the hinges so that the front wall panel will close completely flush with the front of the house and the corner seams will look like all the others. To recess the hinge, mark the position of the hinge, remove it, and gently file a notch that's in from the edge of the hinged panel. To avoid filing away too much wood, test-fit the hinges and the panel several times. The hinge can also be recessed in the fixed wall, where it will be easy to hide with paint or wallpaper.

Install the hinges on the moving panel first, then attach them to the fixed wall. Test the action of the panel and be sure it is working smoothly before painting or sealing the dollhouse shell.

Few kits include latches to hold the hinged wall closed. The larger magnetic latches used for kitchen cabinets work well for this purpose. Locate the latch on the inside corner between the outer wall and the floor of the second story. Paint the latch to match the interior, and it will be hard to spot inside the dollhouse.

JOINING TWO-PIECE WALLS

Some dollhouses have two-piece walls where the upper portion must be abutted to the lower. Edge-to-edge joints like this will always be weak unless they are reinforced with a piece of plywood on the back, but that can interfere with the interior walls and floors. You can make the joint more secure if you glue the roof firmly to the walls, which helps to hold the extension piece in place.

To keep the two-piece wall intact while the shell is put together, add a 1 x 1 or 1 x 2 reinforcing "splint" to the wall until the assembly is complete and the glue is dry. Clamp the splint to the wall with three C-clamps, or use masking tape, wrapped through the windows, to bind the splint to the walls. (See Fig. 4-6.) When all the nails that attach the roof to this wall are in place and the glue is dry, the splint can be removed.

ADDING THE ROOF

The roof panels are a bit more difficult to assemble than the walls. You could let gravity help hold the walls together by turning the box-shaped building on its side so you can drive the nails straight down, but the roof panels all fit at an angle.

Start with the main roof pieces. Tape them together so they stay in place, and make sure the overhang is the same on both ends. If necessary, change the position of the two pieces that meet at the eaves so the overhang at the front and rear is equal. Use this same procedure to install the roof panels on any of the gables. If there are any hinged roof panels, they must be positioned as described for the hinged wall panels.

Clamping the Roof

When you are satisfied with the position of the roof panels, tape them securely in place using the masking-tape-as-clamp technique. This is the same method used to hold the walls

Fig. 4-6. Clamp a 1 x 1 stick through the windows to hold a two-piece wall until the glue dries.

together for marking them and assembling them with glue and nails. Start the strip of tape at least 9 inches onto the panel that is overlapping the exposed end-grain of the one it will join. (See Fig. 4-7.) Press the full length of the tape firmly onto the plywood. Pull the tape tightly over the edge of the first panel and across the second panel. (See Fig. 4-8.) Finally, pull the tape all the way down the second panel and wrap it under the edge. Pulling pressure will be maintained by the second edge, and you can then press the tape firmly onto the second panel. (See Fig. 4-9.)

It takes much longer to describe this process than it does to do it. Once you've had some practice, you can lay the tape onto the roof about as quickly as you can pull it.

Use the same technique to clamp the side and top panels of a mansard roof in place. Start

Fig. 4-7. *Start the masking-tape "clamp" on the over-lapping piece of plywood.*

Fig. 4-8. *Pull the tape tightly over the adjoining piece of plywood.*

Fig. 4-9. *Tape all the roof ridge joints before pushing in the nails.*

Fig. 4-10. *Apply the masking-tape clamps to the near-vertical edges of mansard-style roofs.*

by lightly taping the pieces together so the roof will be self-standing. Use more force and at least two additional pieces of tape to firmly clamp each of the joints. (See Fig. 4-10.) You can now use the technique described earlier for the walls to nail the mansard roof panels together.

Nailing the Roof

When the roof is taped firmly in place, recheck the overhang at the front, back and both sides. Make adjustments to center the roof. Where each peaked wall is joined by the roof, mark the underside of the roof panels for the full length of each wall. (See Fig. 4-11.) Make a line on both the inside and outside of each wall-to-roof joint. Also, make small marks on the underside of the roof where you want to place each nail.

Make some small notes and arrows right on the top of the roof (shingles will later cover your marks) to indicate where each panel fits so you can install them in precisely the same positions. Be particularly careful about clearly marking overlapping and adjoining panels so they do not get flipped end-for-end when you replace them.

Remove the roof panels. Use the no-split technique, described earlier for the walls, to drive a nail or an awl point through the roof at each of the nail locations. (See Fig. 4-12.) Drive nails into each of these holes from the inner surface of each roof panel, just deep enough so $\frac{1}{32}$ inch or less of their points protrudes through the wood. Remove the nails, then replace them by driving them just through the plywood from the outside surface.

With the nails still in place, test-fit the roof panels again, to see if any nails have missed the center of the tops of the walls. Remove the panels and drive new nails wherever necessary.

Spread a thick bead of glue across the tops of the peaked ends of the roof, and tape all the panels firmly back in place. The nails can now be driven in with a few light hammer taps. (See Fig. 4-13.) Leave the dollhouse alone for a day, which gives the glue time to dry. Then remove the tape.

Any dormers must also be assembled, but nails aren't necessary here. Apply a thick bead of glue to each joint, assemble the parts and hold them together with masking tape until the glue dries. It's a good idea to assemble each dormer right on the roof to be certain that the walls are vertical and the roof of the dormer joins firmly against the main roof. Use masking tape to hold the dormer onto the roof while you glue it in place.

Removable Roofs

If your dollhouse has a peaked or mansard-style roof over the tallest tower or turret, do not glue the roof base to the walls. Most of these dollhouse types have a base that supports the roof

Fig. 4-11. Mark the inner and outer edges of the walls on the underside of the roof panels.

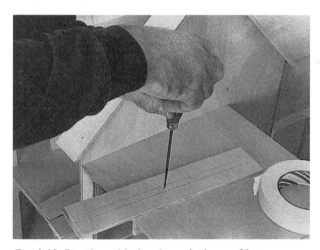

Fig. 4-12. Punch nail holes through the roof between the pencil lines.

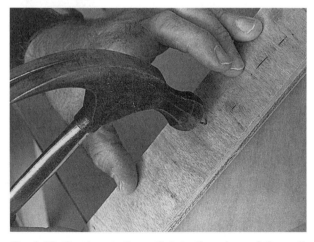

Fig. 4-13. Gently tap the nails into the edges of the wall.

Fig. 4-14. The Walmer "Peaches and Cream" dollhouse, from Chapter 1, is shown here in the bare plywood shell stage of construction.

Fig. 4-15. The interior wall of "Peaches and Cream" can be located on the left side of the stairwell.

Fig. 4-16. The interior wall can also be placed to the right of the stairwell.

itself, so you can finish the roof and then glue it firmly to that base.

The tower or turret roof is often the most vulnerable part of the dollhouse. Instead of gluing, allow that roof to merely rest on the walls, even when the dollhouse is completely finished. If the roof is accidentally bumped during cleaning or moving, it will probably just shift rather than break. This removable tower roof also makes it much easier to move the dollhouse from room to room or in and out of a van.

INSTALLING THE STAIRS

To be sure the stairs fit, this is the time to assemble them. Stairs supplied with the kit should pose no problem, but it's still a good idea to check before you glue the interior walls in place. (See Fig. 4-14, Fig. 4-15 and Fig. 4-16.) If you plan to upgrade the kit with more ornate stairs or install a curved set or a landing, fit all those pieces now. You won't cement them in place until the walls and ceilings are completed. It's also much, much easier to paint the stairs as a separate part before they're installed.

INSTALLING THE INTERIOR WALLS

Decide on the size and location of each room before you install the interior walls. (See Fig. 4-17 on page 40.) The only interior walls that should be glued in place right now are those that help support the stairs. You may decide to make the stairs start on the right of the lower-story wall and emerge on the left of the upper-story wall. True, that's not the way it's done in a real house, but that simple change in position may be just what is needed to "find" enough room for a downstairs entryway and an upstairs bathroom.

The interior wall panels in the attic help to

Fig. 4-17. Decide on the size and location of each room before you install the interior walls.

Fig. 4-18. Real Good Toys' "Woodstock" is ready for the installation of the windows and clapboard siding included in the kit.

support the roof, so they should be glued and nailed in place at this stage of construction. The remaining interior panels can merely be glued in place; nails aren't necessary. Use a try square to be certain that the inner walls are precisely vertical and perfectly parallel to the outer walls. Make any alignment adjustments while the glue is still wet. Before the glue hardens, use a wet rag to remove any excess glue so fillets do not form at the joints.

In some of the smaller dollhouses, there are no other interior walls to install. The larger ones, like Real Good Toys' two-story "Woodstock," may have three or four walls that can be positioned wherever you like (or left out entirely). Consider placing one or more of the shortest walls at a right angle to the others (parallel to the open rear of the house). This will give you the ability to create a shallow room area, like a hallway and an adjacent bathroom.

BUILDING A FOUNDATION

The foundation or simulated basement walls can be the final addition to a shell. If the dollhouse does not have a foundation, you can make one from 1 x 2- or ½ x 2-inch wood strips placed on edge. The strips should be recessed about ¼ inch

from the face of the walls of the shell. You will probably be adding textures to both the walls and the foundation, so that recess should still exist when the dollhouse is completed.

Turn the dollhouse upside down and glue the foundation pieces to the bottom of the floor. You can use plenty of glue because any inside fillets will never be visible.

THE FINISHED DOLLHOUSE SHELL

The dollhouse shell should now be ready for the exterior and interior surface finishes. (See Fig. 4-18.) You may decide to apply stain, paint, simulated board-and-batten or stucco, as described in Chapter 2, or you may want to cover the walls with clapboard siding (see Chapter 5) or with brick or stone (see Chapter 6).

If you feel this carpenter's job is beyond your talents, ask your dollhouse dealer what he or she would charge for an assembled shell. You may find that the extra money offsets the extra effort of assembly. Once the shell is assembled, the remaining exterior and interior finishing is easy enough for dollhouse hobbyists of all skill levels.

FINISHING
THE
EXTERIOR

CHAPTER FIVE

WOOD EXTERIORS

You've got plenty of options for creating a dollhouse exterior that looks like real wood. You might use a stain and a clear covering to create the appearance of furniture. Or you could paint with bright colors so the dollhouse looks like a toy. Finally, you might finish the exterior so it replicates a real home.

SPECIAL EFFECTS

It's possible to duplicate any type of wood exterior in miniature. Some full-size modern houses actually have plywood walls just like a dollhouse shell. These surfaces often have milled lines to look like joints between boards; you can simulate the lines by slicing light vertical creases into the wood with a hobby knife, guided by a steel ruler.

A few shacks and industrial buildings are covered with wood boards placed edge to edge. That effect can be duplicated by covering the exterior with ¹⁄₁₆-inch sheets of scribed wood from Northeastern Scale Models and using the installation techniques for clapboard siding described later in this chapter. Northeastern also offers milled-wood sheets that duplicate the Novelty style that was common on many homes around the turn of the century. Board-and-batten and rustic log exterior finishes are described in Chapter 2.

The choice of exterior finish does not, of course, dictate how you will finish and furnish the interior. There's no reason why a furniture-style dollhouse can't house a set of scale model "lived-in" rooms furnished right down to work-ing table lamps, an ashtray and an open book. Conversely, a realistic exterior can house rooms full of whimsical furniture or even a collection of antique toy furniture. There are no rules here.

CLAPBOARD EXTERIORS

Clapboard is the type of siding that has real boards running horizontally, with the top edge of each board covered by the bottom edge of the board above it. A cross-section view of a clapboard exterior would look like a saw blade.

Most dollhouse kits include a clapboard exterior. (Or you can buy a special finishing kit with precut clapboard panels.) These panels can be installed almost as quickly as you can apply glue because they're already properly sized.

Some of the die-cut ¹⁄₈-inch plywood dollhouse kits include individual wood boards, cut from a single-ply or veneer, that are to be cemented in place, one board at a time, just like real clapboards. Packages of those boards are available from Greenleaf Products. This is a time-consuming process, but it allows you to accurately duplicate the joining ends of real clapboards. You'll see how to cover these die-cut plywood kits with 3¼-inch-wide milled-wood clapboard panels later in this chapter.

Some of the medium-priced dollhouses, saw-cut from ³⁄₈-inch plywood, have the clapboards milled right into the walls. You can simply assemble the shell, paint it, then install the windows and trim.

The most common type of clapboard for dollhouses are milled-wood panels designed to be

Fig. 5-1. Mark the locations for the bottom row of clapboard siding.

Fig. 5-2. The bottom edge of the siding must be perfectly
parallel with the foundation.

glued over a plywood shell. Many kits have special finishing packages available that include the
panels with precut openings for windows and
doors. Just glue the clapboard panels in place in
the sequence shown in the instructions. Paint
the dollhouse, then install the windows, doors
and trim.

Milled-wood panels of simulated clapboard,
about 3½ inches wide and 24 inches long, are
available from Northeastern Scale Models,
Midwest and Houseworks. Northeastern and
Midwest also have 36-inch-long pieces. The simulated boards are offered in choices of ¼-, ⅜- or
½-inch widths to produce 3-, 4½ or 6-inch boards
in l/12 scale. Northeastern also offers 3½ x 24-
inch sheets of ⅜- and ½-inch-width clapboard
siding, with the outer corners rounded to produce the beaded clapboard style of woodwork.
Each of these panels must be cut to fit the walls,
and the window or door openings cut out, as
illustrated later in this chapter.

PURCHASING CLAPBOARD SHEATHING

Milled-wood panels make it much easier and
quicker to cover the walls with clapboard siding
than by applying one board at a time. Basically,
all you're doing is covering the exterior of the
shell with 3¼-inch-wide wood sheets. Each

sheet is milled so it looks like nine individual
boards.

The sheets with the boards milled ⅜ inch
apart should be right for a l/12-scale dollhouse.
You will need to purchase enough of the 3¼ x 24-
inch panels to cover every square inch of the
exterior. Multiply the width by the height (to the
tops of any eaves) of each wall, then add the
results together to find the total number of
square inches. Each of the 24-inch panels has
about 72 square inches of wood. Divide the total
number of square inches on the exterior surfaces
by 72 to determine how many panels to purchase.

It's difficult to join the panels end to end
without creating a glaring seam, so buy enough
of the panels to cover the full width of any of the
walls. If you have many 16- to 18-inch-wide
walls, it might be wise to use the 36-inch-long
panels (with 108 square inches) from Northeastern or Midwest to minimize the leftover scrap.
The 36-inch lengths are also useful for covering
very long dollhouse walls. These panels are
designed to overlap vertically, so all the horizontal seams are automatically hidden.

INSTALLING THE PANELS

Take a good look at the pieces of milled clapboard. The taper on each board is supposed to

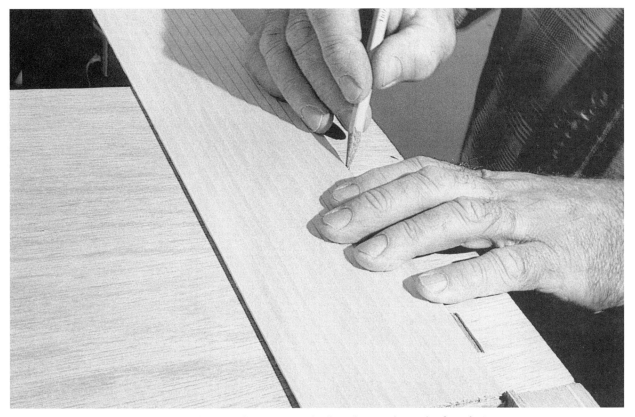

Fig. 5-3. Hold the first sheet of clapboard siding against the line drawn above the foundation.

slope outward at the bottom. Watch carefully, as you cut and install each piece, to be certain it is facing the proper direction.

The milled-wood clapboard siding works well on any dollhouse. For the photographs, I used Greenleaf's "Arthur." Greenleaf suggests that any siding be applied after the window frames are in place. Frankly, that's just too much work. Each piece of siding must be carefully cut to match the shape of the window frames exactly—there's no room for error and no place to hide any mistakes.

I suggest that you cover the walls with sheathing, then add the window frames and trim. That way, you can also prepaint the frames and trim to avoid hand-painting.

The exterior wall covering system shown here allows plenty of room for errors and slightly uneven cuts. One end of each milled-wood section is covered by a window or door frame and the other end by a piece of corner trim. Still, be

as careful as possible so you don't make a mistake you cannot cover.

For ease of working, turn the plywood shell so the wall you are going to cover is facing upward. Place some 2 x 4 blocks beneath the opposite wall so the dollhouse doesn't rest on the edges of the roof.

The "Arthur" has no foundation or basement, so simulate one by starting the first row of clapboards about 1⅜ inches from the bottom. That's also about the height of the porch, so the foundation can extend right out to the porch. Measure carefully and make a mark near the front and another near the rear of each wall. Lay a steel ruler along the marks and draw a pencil line across the bottom of each wall. (See Fig. 5-1 and Fig. 5-2.) That line will be the baseline for installing the siding.

Hold a piece of the milled-wood clapboard siding against the pencil mark. Place one end flush with the end of the wall. (See Fig. 5-3.)

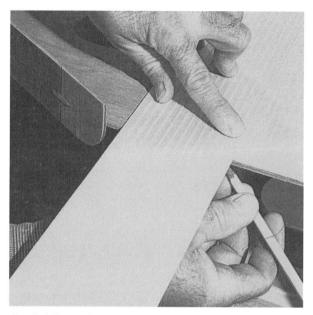

Fig. 5-4. Trace the edge of the wall on the back side of the clapboard.

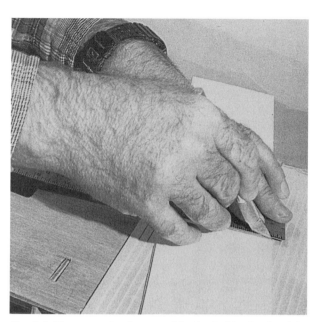

Fig. 5-5. Use a steel ruler to guide the hobby knife while you cut the siding.

Fig. 5-6. Break the clapboard siding along the knife cut by bending it over the steel ruler.

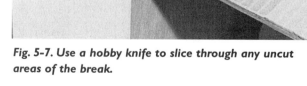

Fig. 5-7. Use a hobby knife to slice through any uncut areas of the break.

Run a pencil line underneath the clapboard on the opposite wall to mark where the clapboard must be cut. (See Fig. 5-4.)

Lift up the clapboard and lay a steel ruler over the pencil line you just drew on the back of the panel. The line will be about 1/32 inch from where you actually want to cut, so move the ruler inward to make the panel that much shorter. Gently slice along the line with an X-Acto number 1 hobby knife and a number 2 blade. Make two or three passes with the knife, and you should find you've cut about halfway through the panel. (See Fig. 5-5.)

Hold the sliced panel over the steel ruler and bend the panel down, away from the cut. (See Fig. 5-6.) The panel will break right along the cut but will leave slivers and wisps of wood. With the panel still bent at a sharp angle, run the hobby knife along the cut to slice through any remaining slivers of wood. (See Fig. 5-7.) Sand the end of the panel with a sanding block to remove any burrs. (See Fig. 5-8.) Using the same procedure, cut the next panel up the wall.

GLUING THE CLAPBOARD TO THE WALLS

The clapboard must be glued securely to the walls or it will warp when painted. Quick Grab cement by 3C seems to work best for holding these wood panels to the dollhouse shell. Before you proceed, however, experiment on a few scraps of milled-wood panel and a scrap of plywood wall to get the feeling for the proper application.

Run a bead of the glue all around the panel, and another all around the area of the plywood wall that the panel will cover. (See Fig. 5-9.) Also, run a wavy line of the glue down the center of the panel, and another over the plywood walls. Push the panel in place immediately, pressing firmly and moving it about an inch from side to side to spread the glue evenly.

Remove the panel for a count of ten. When you replace it, start with the bottom edge aligned and the sides of the panel in line with the edges of the plywood. You won't be able to move the panel more than about ⅛ inch this time, so get it in the proper position. Press the panel down firmly with both hands.

Try to lift the panel at this moment. You should see small hairs of glue gripping both the panel and the wall—that's just the right amount of tackiness for the glue to set completely. (See Fig. 5-10 on page 48.) If the glue is too runny, it may not dry. If it's too dry, it may not hold as firmly.

If you do apply the panel before the glue is dry enough, let it sit for a few days before you paint it. If you waited too long and the glue

Fig. 5-8. Use a sanding block to smooth the cut end.

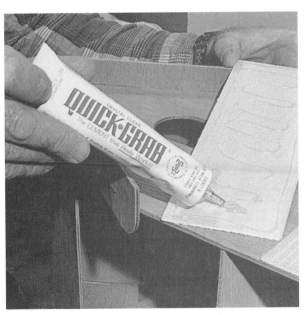

Fig. 5-9. Apply wavy beads of Quick Grab cement to the back of the siding.

won't stick firmly, apply another layer of glue to both the plywood and the milled-wood panel and repeat the process.

On the dollhouse itself, carefully align the

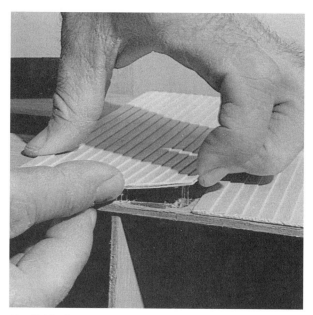

Fig. 5-10. Gently lift the edge of the clapboard to test the glue.

Fig. 5-11. Mark the location of the window edges on the back side of the clapboard.

Fig. 5-12. Use several light strokes with the hobby knife to cut any curved window openings.

bottom and side edges of the first panel on the house. When you add the second panel, be sure that the edges overlap and the angle of the milled clapboards flows outward at the bottom.

CUTTING WINDOW AND DOOR OPENINGS

When the clapboard panels cover a window or door, the opening must be cut before you glue the panel to the plywood. Cut the panel to length, then hold it in place over the window. Mark the position of the window on the back of the clapboard panel. (See Fig. 5-11.) Remove the panel and turn it over. Use a steel ruler to guide the hobby knife as you cut along the marked line. The cut can be shallow and the window broken out of the panel, just as when cutting the panel to length. If the top of the window is curved, however, you must cut clear through. It should take only about five or six passes to slice through the soft wood. (See Fig. 5-12.)

When you are satisfied with the window opening, glue the clapboard in place as described above. After the glue has set, trim around the edges with a hobby knife to remove any clapboard that may protrude into the window opening. Test-fit the window and, if necessary, trim

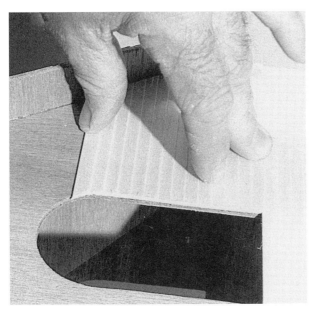

Fig. 5-13. *Test-fit the panels around the window.*

Fig. 5-14. *Whittle away small errors in the size of the window openings after the clapboard is glued to the wall.*

away more of the clapboard until you get a perfect fit. (See Fig. 5-13, Fig. 5-14 and Fig. 5-15.)

FITTING CLAPBOARD BENEATH THE EAVES

When you have covered the walls high enough to be under the eaves of a peaked roof, lay the clapboard right on the overhanging edges of the roof. Look directly down on the wall so you can align the bottom edge of the clapboard with the last piece that you glued to the wall. Hold the clapboard firmly and place a steel ruler on top of it while you draw a line to indicate the location of the wall, just beneath the roof. Draw the locations of both eaves. (See Fig. 5-16 on page 50.)

Remove the clapboard and cut along the pencil lines. To be sure the cut piece fits, lay it in place on the wall. If you are careful enough when you look down on the clapboard as you mark it, the piece should fit precisely.

If a leftover triangle of clapboard protrudes past the edge of the wall, mark the back of the clapboard and cut off the excess material. When you are satisfied with the fit, glue the clapboard in place. The leftover pieces can be used to fill in any small areas near the peak of the roof.

An alternative technique for fitting the clap-

Fig. 5-15. *Small nicks or gouges like this will be hidden by the window frames.*

Fig. 5-16. Hold the clapboard against the eaves and mark the edges of the roof.

board siding beneath the eaves of a peaked roof is to make a paper pattern of the area to be covered. Transfer the pattern to the clapboard, cut the clapboard, and install. The techniques for making paper patterns are shown in Chapter 14.

PAINTING CLAPBOARD SIDING

You can use any of the latex interior house paints or try the special Builder's Choice, Deco Art Americana or Borden's Accent paints to cover the milled-wood clapboard. To make the job easy, use a brush the same width as the clapboards.

The first coat of paint will likely raise a lot of the wood grain. Let the paint dry for at least 24 hours before you sand the surface with a fine-grit sandpaper. Keep the sandpaper away from the crisp edges of the boards—only the faces of the boards need to be smoothed. An emery board is just about the same width as the clapboards, so it

makes an excellent sanding tool. Buy a few packages of emery boards so you'll have plenty; they tend to clog quickly.

Wipe the walls clean with a damp rag before applying a second coat of paint. Two or three coats should give a smooth finish while still allowing some of the grain to show.

WEATHERING AND ANTIQUING

The thought of intentionally making a bright, shiny new dollhouse appear old or used may strike you as appalling, but truly realistic dollhouse scenes are creating more and more interest. Bill Lankford's two-story brick store, shown in the color section, has a back wall of weathered clapboard. That same antique look can be achieved with a clapboard structure.

The secret for creating a realistic model is to

duplicate the colors and details of the real thing. This is not the place to let your imagination rule. Seek out a "model" full-size building—it doesn't need to be anything like your miniature except in color and age—and take color photographs of it from several different angles.

Real clapboards are only 12 feet long—that's 12 inches on a dollhouse. If any of your walls are longer than that, there is good reason to simulate the end joints in the clapboard. Since this is a model, I'd suggest simulating joints on any wall area that is just 8 inches wide. That means that the ends of boards can be simulated above and below most windows.

To simulate the end of a board, simply draw a thin line down one of the boards with a fine-point felt-tip pen, guided by a ruler. Stagger the joints by drawing a line down one board 2 inches in from the right wall. On the next board, draw a line 8 inches in from the right wall.

If you want to exaggerate the weathering, use the pen to make two small dots on either side of each line, suggesting nail heads. To replicate a really old building, draw short streaks of "rust" running down from those nail heads with a brown fine-point felt-tip pen.

The lines will be a bit too visible, so blend them into the overall wall color by brushing a thin "wash" of the main color over the clapboards. Mix about four parts water to one part paint to make the wash. Apply it with a ⅜-inch-wide brush, just as you did when painting the clapboards.

To age the wood, mix one part white into the wash for a more pastel version of the original color. This can be used in place of the wash suggested above. Apply this wash with brush strokes running up and down the wall. You'll create the effect of sun-bleached paint being washed down the walls by rain.

You can "dirty" up your dollhouse with some "dust" using a dark brown (burnt umber) artist's pastel chalk to simulate the wind- and rain-blown dirt and smoke that stick to the walls. Regular pastels won't work because they contain too much oil. If you cannot find pastel chalks, use a piece of artist's charcoal. Rub the chalk or charcoal on a piece of fine-grit sandpaper, reducing it to a powder. Store the powder in a jar with a screw-on lid.

Use a ¾-inch-wide soft-bristled brush to spread the powder over the wall. Apply a bit more near the bottom, where rain will have splashed up dirt. Apply more of the dust under the eaves of the roof and under the bottoms of the window lintels. Brush some around the window frames and anywhere else that dirt might accumulate. Again, study photographs of a real building to see where the dirt builds up. If you apply too much, take it off with a wet rag or apply another coat of wash. When you're satisfied, cover all the clear window glazing with paper masks, and spray the wall with clear flat paint to preserve the dusty appearance. If you're not satisfied with the results, paint the walls the original color and start over. It takes some practice because you are really learning an art—the art of weathering.

CHAPTER SIX

BRICK AND STONE EXTERIORS

It's simple enough to finish a wooden doll-house so it looks like wood. Finishing that same structure to look like brick would seem to be a bit more difficult, but it's really just as easy. You don't lay brick after brick; you simply apply a sheathing of real or simulated brick, just as you would "build" clapboard siding with wood sheathing.

Many commercial products allow you to simulate brick or stone on dollhouse walls, chimneys and fireplaces, foundations and patios, porches and sidewalks. Whatever technique you choose, always tilt the dollhouse, so the wall to be covered with brick or stone is horizontal, when applying or painting the surface. Support the wall nearest the floor with some 2 x 4 blocks so the weight of the dollhouse does not rest on the edges of the roof.

THE MAGIC-BRIK SYSTEM

Dee's Delights' Magic-Brik (as well as Magic-Ston and Magic Slat) system is perhaps the easiest way to create brick or stone textures. There's a photo of this process in the color section. The system is simple enough: First, paint the walls with a gray mortar-colored latex wall paint and let that dry overnight. Second, press the mortar mask tape (included with the kit) over the mortar. The mask can be pulled right around corners, so no special corner treatment is needed. Third, use a disposable stiff-bristled brush to cover the mask with a thick layer of the putty-like compound (Magic-Brik). Finally, pull off the

mask to reveal the mortar lines. (See Fig. 6-1.) For a free-standing chimney on a roof, apply the brick or stone finish; then simply place the finished chimney on top of the roof shingles. (See

Fig. 6-1. The three steps in applying Magic-Ston: The mortar mask is applied (top), then the "stone" compound is brushed over the surface to completely bury the mortar mask (center), and the mortar mask is removed (bottom).

Fig. 6-2. Paint the chimney as a separate piece and rest it on top of the shingles.

Fig. 6-2.) The same procedure is used to apply the Magic-Ston, Magic-Bloc and Magic-Slat compounds as well. (See Fig. 6-3.).

CREATING REALISM

Magic-Brik (as well as Magic-Bloc) is available in red or white. Since the compound is the color and texture of brick, no additional painting is required. The results will be much more realistic, however, if you mix a paint using about four parts water to one part medium-gray latex wall paint. Brush this "wash" over the entire Magic-Brik wall to subdue the mortar lines and blend them into the brick.

The differences in the colors of real bricks are usually quite subtle, so painting about one brick in ten a shade darker or lighter further enhances the realism of your dollhouse. To lighten a brick, dip a rag in thinner, wrap it around

your fingertip and scrub off the mortar wash. To make a brick darker, mix about 2 ounces of water and 1 ounce of dark brown or burnt umber acrylic paint. Use a number 2 paint brush to apply this wash to about one brick in twenty, but first test it on a scrap of the Magic-Brik color to be sure it's not too dark or light. You may want to add a bit more water or color to the mix.

SIMULATING USED BRICKS

Many full-size houses are built or accented with used bricks in a variety of colors, from almost black to light beige. Unfortunately, the only way to simulate the effect of so many random colors is to paint one brick at a time. Start with the procedures outlined above to impart a brick-and-mortar color to the entire wall. Buy a few more bottles of paint that have the same color value as the original Magic-Brik but with more black,

Fig. 6-3. On this dollhouse, the brick surfaces are Magic-Brik and the stone is Magic-Ston.

more yellow and more red. Also, mix two more bottles of paint for washes, one black and the other light, consisting of about four parts water to one part acrylic paint.

Use a number 2 brush to apply these alternate colors to individual bricks. You can probably achieve the variegated effect you want by painting only about one brick in five, so the process isn't quite as tedious as it might sound.

PLASTIC BRICK AND STONE SHEETS

Textured plastic sheets are manufactured by heating and embossing the sheets. The master patterns are carefully carved both with a milling machine and by hand to create very realistic bricks or stones and mortar seams. All of that detail is captured when a vacuum pulls the heat-

ed plastic tightly over a mold; hence, you have the term "vacuum-formed" plastic brick sheets.

Holgate and Reynolds makes thick, beige-colored sheets of bricks or concrete blocks, while Precision Products uses white styrene plastic for vacuum-formed textures. Precision offers a choice of new or rough brick, coursed or random stone, and stone or concrete blocks. Plastruct has sheets of brick, fieldstone, random fieldstone, dressed stone and concrete block.

JR Enterprises and Miniature House offer prepainted vacuum-formed plastic brick sheets. JR has a standard red brick as well as yellow or gray, each with a choice of gray or black mortar. JR also offers the excellent Medley series of painted bricks with a random array of darker individual bricks, available in brick red, dark brick red, gray and yellow, each with medium gray mortar. Miniature House has prepainted red bricks. (See Fig. 6-4 on page 56.)

Fig. 6-4. The Precision Products vacuum-formed bricks can be painted to match any brick color. The panels are available for both half-scale (shown) and 1/12 scale.

PAINTING THE SHEETS

It's easiest to paint the bricks or stones before the plastic sheets are attached to the dollhouse. You can probably find the color you want in a bottle of acrylic paint at a hobby store that sells supplies for model railroads. Badger's Accu-Flex and Floquil's Polly S paints are both acrylics, and they offer a number of reddish-brown colors similar to most shades of brick.

Dip a moist rag into the paint and rub it lightly over the plastic sheet. Work carefully, and the color will touch only the bricks. The paint will skip right over the mortar lines, leaving them the original color. (See Fig. 6-5.)

RECREATING BRICK COLORS

To achieve a realistic variegated effect, mix two more small bottles of brick color. Into each bottle, pour about an ounce of the same color you

just wiped over the walls. Add a few drops of the same brand of black paint to one bottle and a few drops of white to the other.

Test the alternative colors on a scrap of the brick plastic; you're looking for a subtle variation in color, not real contrast. When you're satisfied, use the colors to paint about one brick in ten in a random pattern. You can simulate the variegated colors of used brick with the techniques described above for Magic-Brik.

The bricks will be more realistic if you subdue the colors with a light gray wash. Mix about four parts water and one part Accu-Flex or Polly S Concrete gray. Brush this wash over the entire sheet to "weather" it and provide a better mortar color between the bricks or stones.

SIMULATING THE LOOK OF STONE

The same painting techniques apply to vacuum-formed plastic sheets of stone and concrete

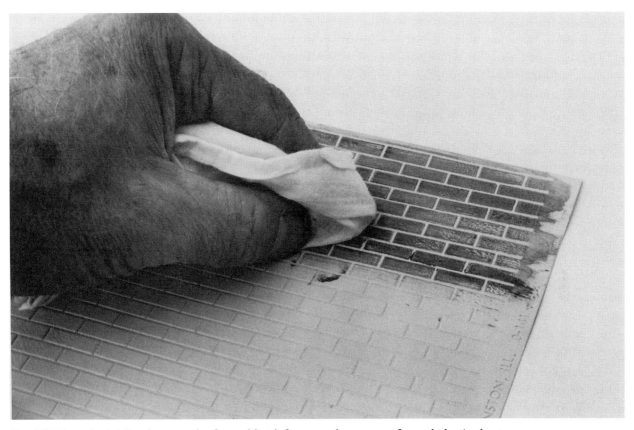

Fig. 6-5. Wipe the brick color over the formed brick faces on the vacuum-formed plastic sheets.

blocks. Stones and blocks, however, usually have shadow effects that aren't visible on the painted plastic. To accent the shading, mix a wash of about one part dark brown or burnt umber acrylic paint to nine parts water. This wash is a bit thinner than the gray one used to blend the mortar colors. Add a few drops of liquid detergent to help break the surface tension so the wash will flow more easily into cracks and crevices.

Brush the dark brown wash over the bricks or stones. The color will run right off the highlights and settle only in the tiny seams, cracks and hollows to create automatic shadows. Let the wash dry completely before you judge its effect. You can apply several coats to achieve the look you want. These techniques also work well with Magic-Ston, Magic-Bloc and Magic-Slat paint-on textures.

INSTALLING PLASTIC SHEETS

Vacuum-formed plastic sheets can be applied to the walls very much like milled-wood clapboard siding. First, place the plastic panel over the wall and mark the edges of the wall on the back of the plastic, using the techniques shown in Chapter 5. Remove the panels and cut along the pencil lines with scissors.

It will take two or more sheets of the brick or stone to cover each wall of the dollhouse. Hold the first sheet in place with masking tape while you cut the additional sheets needed to cover a wall. When you position the second sheet, be sure that the bottom row of bricks is offset a half-brick width from the first brick sheet. Mark that second sheet and cut it to size. Cut enough of the brick sheets to completely cover the wall.

Use clear silicone bathtub caulking compound to install the panels. Spread a bead of the silicone around the edge of the dollhouse wall

Fig. 6-6. Align the mortar marks at the corners when applying the vacuum-formed plastic brick sheets.

and another wavy bead through the center of the wall. There's no need to put any on the panel. Press the plastic brick panel onto the wall and line up all the edges. Stack some books on the panel to hold it firmly to the wall and let it dry overnight.

These plastic sheets can also be installed with double-stick carpet tape, so long as the plywood walls have been sealed and painted with two or three color coats to provide a smooth surface. Lay strips of tape around all the edges of any windows and doors and along all four edges of the walls. Apply more strips of tape to produce a grid effect of 4 x 4-inch squares.

The plastic sheet must be carefully positioned, starting at the two lower corners. Curl the sheet upward as you begin to lay it, so only the lower edge and the two lower corners are touching the edge of the dollhouse. Slowly unroll the sheet, working up the wall and pressing firmly with both hands to force the plastic sheet down on the tape. Finally, go over the face of the sheet with a new paint roller to anchor the plastic firmly to the tape.

CUTTING WINDOW AND DOOR OPENINGS

With a hobby knife, cut the window and door openings from inside the dollhouse; use the edge of each window or door opening to guide the blade. Make three or four light cuts. When you have sliced all around the window, gently wiggle the plastic in and out. It will soon begin to snap along the sliced lines.

If you are very careful, you may be able to line up the mortar lines on the first surface so they align perfectly with those on the adjacent

Fig. 6-7. Scribe a line on the real brick where you want it to break.

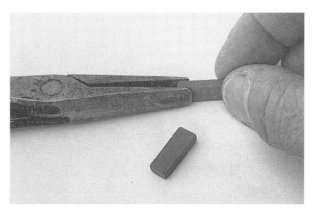

Fig. 6-8. Use pliers to hold the shortest end of the brick.

USING REAL BRICKS

Dollhouses are just large enough to make it possible to use real-world materials for many of the components. Fine-grained woods, for example, produce the effect of typical hardwoods reduced to 1/12-scale. You can also obtain bricks molded from much finer clay than full-size bricks so they are incredibly realistic.

Houseworks and Miniature House offer real bricks on 6 x 12-inch sheets of cloth mesh. These "gang brick" sheets can be applied much more quickly and easily to a wall, chimney or foundation than by laying one brick at a time.

CREATING CORNERS

The corners are the only tough part of applying individual bricks. Decide which corner treatment you will use before you apply the sheets of real brick: You can use Houseworks' injection-molded plastic corners with bricks that match the size and color of the real bricks, or you can break individual bricks and fit them to the corners.

To install the Houseworks 8207 Brickmaster plastic corners, simply hold the corner piece in place and mark where to cut it. Use a razor saw to cut between the simulated mortar lines. You may need to fill in at the top with trim to hide a "missing" half-row of bricks. Glue the corner to the dollhouse with clear silicone bathtub caulking compound.

surface. Cut the bricks so they overlap at the ends and appear to be running right around the corner. (See Fig. 6-6.) John Hutt applied Precision's vacuum-formed plastic brick, stone, wood and shingle sheets to a half-scale Greenleaf "Fairfield" dollhouse using these techniques. There's a photograph of his dollhouse in the color section.

The corners can also be covered with special corner strips, much like the wood trim on a clapboard-covered dollhouse, to hide any ragged edges. Use a hobby knife to cut around each of the bricks on the strips and remove them from the plastic sheet. Hold the corner strip over a sharp square board or countertop and bend it at a right angle midway along the bricks.

Use clear silicone bathtub caulking compound to cement the corner piece over the brick-covered walls. For a crisp corner, glue just one-half of the strip to one wall and hold it down with some books until the silicone sets, then turn the dollhouse 90 degrees. Lift the edge of the brick corner piece and spread some silicone. Press the edge down and weight it with books until the silicone sets. Repeat the process with each corner.

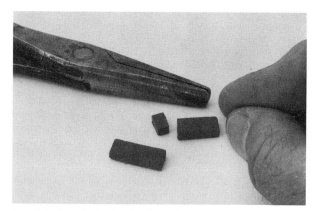

Fig. 6-9. Break the brick along that scribed line.

Fig. 6-10. The two bottom bricks are full bricks. The top pieces are the two portions of a broken brick.

To make real brick corners, slice lightly along the brick with a hobby knife. (See Fig. 6-7 on page 59.) Hold the brick with pliers and bend it down. (See Fig. 6-8 on page 59.) The brick will break along the line. (See Fig. 6-9.)

The pattern shown here allows you to run the sheets of brick right up to the corner. The shortest of the broken bricks goes back on the sheet, and the longer broken brick goes on the adjacent wall, just one row above or below the short brick. This puts all the short bricks on one wall at the corner and all the long bricks on the other wall. (Fig. 6-10.)

BUILDING A WALL

If you are using the Houseworks 8207 plastic brick corners, install just one of them. Lay the sheet in place, with the bricks interlocked with the corner. Add other sheets as necessary to run the bricks all across the wall.

Note how the ends of the bricks line up with the second corner. You may get lucky and find that they interlock nicely with the second corner piece. If not, you may have to make a whole row of half-length bricks to get them to interlock with the second corner piece.

If you're using the "broken brick" technique described earlier, the sheet of bricks can be run right up to the edge of the corner. Cut the visible mesh from between the end bricks with a hobby knife. (See Fig. 6-11.) You can probably

Fig. 6-11. Shear the mesh backing with scissors to cut the sheets of brick to the proper size.

find a combination of full and broken bricks to adjust the pattern to fill the wall right up to the second corner.

Run the sheet of bricks as close to the window and door openings as possible, then mark the places where the sheet must be cut to clear windows and doors. You'll no doubt have to break individual bricks to get close enough to the openings. Test-fit each window or door, with

Fig. 6-12. Cement the bricks to the wall or foundation with silicone bathtub caulking compound.

Fig. 6-13. Brush the mortar mix between the bricks after they are glued to the wall.

the brick panels in place, so you can see how much of the frame hides any missing bricks. Use broken bricks to fill in the gaps that will be visible when the windows and doors are installed.

Both the individual bricks and sheets can be held in place with clear silicone bathtub caulking compound. (See Fig. 6-12.) To avoid smearing the bricks, apply the compound only to the plywood walls. The entire wall area must be covered with the silicone, so run some wavy beads and use a scrap of wood as a squeegee to spread an even layer. The silicone dries quickly, so apply it only to areas where you have all the bricks cut, fitted and ready to install. If you do get silicone on a brick's face, scrape it off with a knife, then sand the brick with medium-grit sandpaper.

REAL MORTAR

The real bricks are really just the outer third—the faces—of a full brick. These shallow bricks are much easier to glue in place than full bricks, and the mortar is only a cosmetic touch. Wall sizing or tile grout can be used for mortar, but both are a bit too white. Miniature House makes gray and white (actually light gray) mortars for dollhouses. Use a ½-inch-wide stiff-bristled brush to spread the mortar between the bricks. (See Fig. 6-13.) Wipe the mortar from the faces of the bricks with a wet rag. Some of that mortar color will remain, providing a realistic weathered

appearance. If you prefer your bricks to look fresh and new, spray them with clear, flat acrylic paint before applying the mortar.

WEATHERING AND ANTIQUING

Real brick and stone take on a weathered appearance almost as soon as they are laid. The painted brick or stone, and even the real clay bricks, on dollhouse walls will likely have too much contrast between the color of the brick or stone and the color of the mortar. For more realism, mix a wash with four parts water and one part gray acrylic paint. Brush this over the bricks or stones with vertical strokes to simulate rain-washed mortar. Bill Lankford's brick store, shown in the color section, is an example of nicely weathered brick and stone.

Older brick walls will appear more faded. To produce that sun-bleached effect, apply a second or even a third coat of the wash. Allow each coat to dry completely because the wash turns a bit more gray after it dries.

Older brick buildings often have a few missing bricks and cracks, a look easily duplicated on real brick walls by removing one of the bricks before the silicone sets. Break the brick and replace it. Cracks can be simulated on painted brick walls with a thin black line applied with fine-point felt-tip marker.

CHAPTER SEVEN

DOORS AND WINDOWS

Doors and windows can define the character of your dollhouse. They may help establish your dollhouse as a whimsical toy, or they can be the focal points of realism that makes your miniature home an accurate scale model.

Doors and windows are, perhaps, the easiest elements of a dollhouse to customize. By simply substituting different windows from those in the kit, you can alter the entire character of the dollhouse.

STANDARD SIZES

The term "standard" sometimes implies that whatever does not conform is suspect. This is certainly not true when referring to doors and windows for dollhouses. The better-quality kits and shells often (but not always) have window and door openings cut to a standard size, and give the consumer the widest possible choice of styles without the need to recut the precut openings. (See Fig. 7-1.)

The standard-size opening for windows is $2\frac{9}{16}$ x $5\frac{1}{16}$ inches. For interior doors, it's 3 x 7 inches. A variety of styles fit comfortably in those openings. Exterior door openings vary considerably, but most manufacturers offer several styles to fit a $3\frac{1}{16}$ x $7\frac{9}{16}$-inch opening.

Accessory doors and windows, as well as those furnished with complete kits or as accessory packs, have frames designed to fit into $\frac{3}{8}$- and $\frac{1}{2}$-inch-thick walls. The lower-cost nonworking windows and the built-up ones assembled from finished precut milled-wood frames are made for $\frac{3}{8}$-inch-thick walls; so are most doors. Working windows and ornate doors are designed to fit

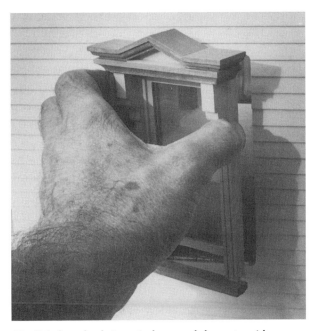

Fig. 7-1. Standard-size windows and doors provide a choice of styles in most dollhouse shells.

into $\frac{1}{2}$-inch-thick walls. It's easy to adapt any window or door to a dollhouse with walls of almost any thickness. It's also possible to enlarge the openings to accommodate standard-size doors and windows.

CUSTOM WINDOWS FOR DIE-CUT KITS

Lower-priced dollhouses have windows that best suit the style of the house. The die-cut $\frac{1}{8}$-inch plywood dollhouses each have their own window

Fig. 7-2. The one-piece shutters, windows and trim are from the inexpensive Walmer kits.

sizes, as do the least expensive ¼- and ⅜-inch plywood dollhouse kits. And neither type is interchangeable with each other or with the standard sizes.

Fortunately, you'll find upgraded windows for most of the lower-priced kits. Timberbrook, for example, makes milled-wood working windows and doors to replace the plywood components in four of the die-cut Greenleaf Products dollhouse kits: "Westville," "Jefferson," "Garfield" and "Pierce." Most other replacement windows, however, are designed with frames for walls at least ⅜ inch thick. That means that a full ¼ inch of the window will protrude inside the walls of a ⅛-inch plywood dollhouse.

The majority of the Greenleaf and Duracraft dollhouse kits have windows that are smaller than the milled-wood replacements, and usually at least one window has a curved top. Exact replacements for those windows would be prohibitively expensive to produce, but you can replace any window or door with the next size up by enlarging the opening. The Timberbrook

windows for the Greenleaf dollhouses would be a wise first choice because they are designed for ⅛-inch plywood walls, but they are not available individually. The thicker custom windows can, however, be shimmed to fit using one of these three techniques:

Install a framework around the inside of the window frame with ¼-inch-square wood so the window protrudes ¼ inch from the wall. You can disguise part of that excessive bulk by covering the exterior walls of the kit with ⅛-inch-thick simulated clapboard, as shown in Chapter 5, or with real bricks, as shown in Chapter 6.

Make a similar framework of ¼-inch-square wood, but put it around the window or door on the inside of the house. It will look like interior window trim that is three times thicker than it should be. Since these ¼-inch-square strips will be visible, cut each of them at a 45-degree angle for more attractive mitered corner joints.

Use ⅛-inch spacers on both the inside and outside of the walls. If you cover the exterior with ⅛-inch-thick clapboard siding or bricks, that will move the window out the first ⅛ inch. Make a framework for the inside using ⅛-inch-square wood, with the corner joints mitered with 45-degree cuts. For more realism, substitute some of the ⅛-inch milled-wood picture-frame mouldings from Northeastern Scale Models to simulate ornate interior window framing.

Custom Windows for Shells

Walmer Dollhouses supplies a simple milled-wood window kit in the lower-priced Lilliput series, including the "Lemon Twist," "Kiwi Cottage" and "Peaches and Cream" kits. These windows have five pieces: the cornice and lintel, two shutters and plastic glazing with printed-on mullions. The shutters incorporate the vertical window trim. (See Fig. 7-2.) Walmer also offers higher-quality assembled replacement windows with milled-wood sides, a wood mullion and ornate cornice, which would also work well in any of the ¼-inch plywood shells.

Virtually all of the nonworking windows are designed to fit ⅜-inch-thick walls. Working windows that open with the panes sliding up and

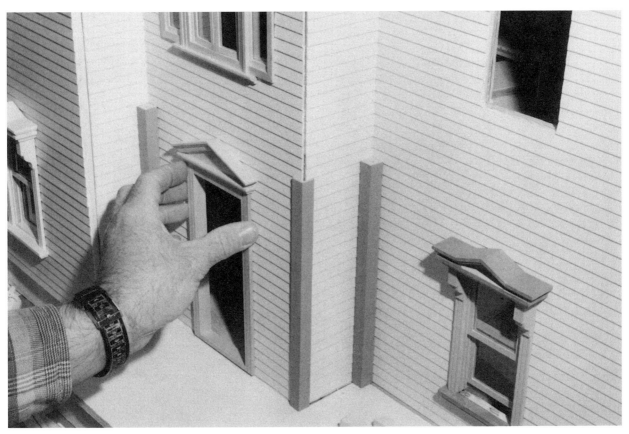

Fig. 7-3. Test-fit each door and window before painting it.

down are designed for ½-inch thick walls. If you start with a ⅜-inch-thick plywood shell and add ⅛ inch of simulated clapboard or real brick to the exterior, the walls are effectively ½ inch thick. The window frames for ⅜-inch-thick walls will not protrude far enough into the interior to join the interior frame of the window, but you can build an extension from ⅛-inch-square wood strips.

Most of these windows and doors include precut wood strips to make interior frames with the corners mitered with 45-degree cuts. Do not install that framework until the wallpaper or other interior wall finishing is complete. In fact, it's best not to install the windows or doors until both the interior and exterior have been painted and finished.

CUTTING NEW OPENINGS

To enlarge an opening or cut a new one, just hold the new window or door precisely where you want it on the outside of the wall. The opening will only need to be large enough to fit the inside frame of the new element. Using a pencil, trace the locations of all four sides of the inside moulding on the wall.

If you are cutting a new opening, begin by drilling a ¼-inch hole near one corner of the penciled rectangle. The blade of an electric saber saw or a hand coping saw can then be inserted in the hole to start the cut. Square off the inside corners using a rectangular wood file or sandpaper wrapped around a scrap of wood.

Test-fit the windows to be certain that they are square with the surrounding walls. (See Fig. 7-3.) If the opening is crooked, saw or file it to

Fig. 7-4. Printed clear plastic "stained glass" is available to fit most standard-size windows.

correct the error. Remember, the frames on the windows extend at least ⅛ inch on all sides, which leaves plenty of room to hide an oversize or crooked opening.

Most of the windows also include inside trim that can hide the oversize opening. Northeastern makes ornate milled-wood interior trim that can be used to upgrade the appearance of any interior or to provide a frame for those windows that do not include one.

MULLIONS AND OTHER DETAILS

Most of the Greenleaf and Duracraft kits and the lower-priced ¼- and ⅜-inch plywood dollhouse kits have the window mullions printed right on the clear plastic glazing. Houseworks has replacement clear plastic mullions with Tudor-

style mullions laser-etched into the surface. You can add similar mullions to any clear window using 1⁄16-inch-wide drafting tape sold by drafting-supply and art-supply stores.

The better-quality replacement windows are available with preassembled wood mullions. A few windows are available with Tudor-style diamond-shaped mullions, preassembled as intricate wood lattices to be laid over the glazing. Some assembled windows include strips of toothpick-size pieces of wood for making mullions.

PLASTIC WINDOW GLAZING

Some of the replacement windows and doors have assembled wooden mullions. These include several of the Colonial styles, most of those with curved upper windows and some French doors. These doors and windows, howev-

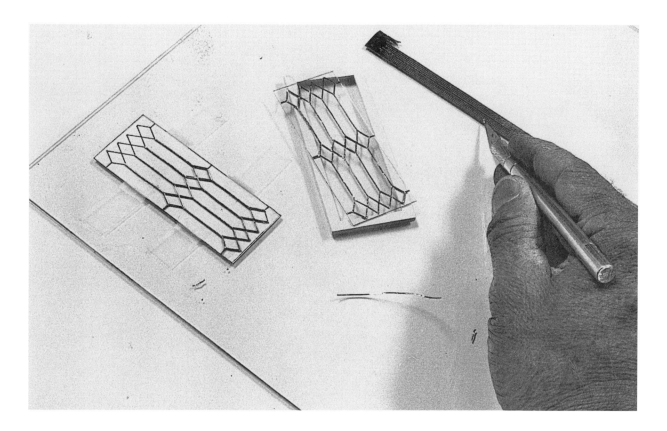

Fig. 7-5. Slice thin strips of self-adhesive lead or copper foil to create "leaded" glass windows.

er, usually lack any clear plastic glazing. Hobby shops sell sheets of clear styrene plastic that can be cut with a hobby knife to provide a pane for each opening. I would suggest making just one window and filing it to exact size, then use it as a pattern for all the others. Hold the window glazing in place by touching the edges with clear silicone bathtub caulking compound.

STAINED-GLASS WINDOWS

Several firms produce clear plastic windows that are printed with full-color stained-glass designs. (See Fig. 7-4.) Houseworks has several sizes of clear plastic panels with the leading for stained glass etched into the surface. Noonmark offers door and window panels with ornate frosted patterns. Woodland Scenics makes dry transfer rub-on decals to simulate leaded and stained glass.

Or if you want, you can create the colors of

stained glass with felt-tipped markers. Use fine-grit sandpaper to sand the clear plastic so the surface has some "tooth," then apply the marker to the roughened side. If the colors are too opaque, let them dry and apply a second coat. A few dollhouse stores have handmade plastic "stained-glass" windows created by a local craftsman.

Dollhouse stores sell sheets of aluminum and (for now) lead with self-stick adhesive backings, which can be easily cut into strips as dividers for leaded and stained-glass windows. (See Fig. 7-5.) If you are working with lead, wear disposable rubber gloves. Use a hobby knife, guided by a steel ruler, to slice the sheet into $\frac{1}{16}$-inch-wide strips. Cut the strips to length and apply them to the clear plastic. Houseworks' etched windows and doors can be upgraded with this technique. With practice, you can slice the lead into $\frac{1}{32}$-inch-wide strips and curve it into intricate stained-glass designs.

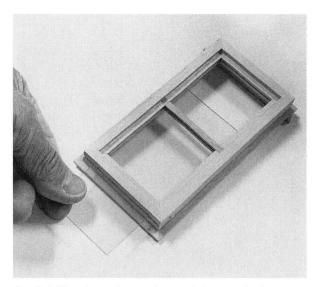

Fig. 7-6. The clear plastic glazing slides out the bottom of most nonworking windows.

Fig. 7-7. Remove the sliding panes from working windows before painting.

HINGED DOORS

Most of the doors in kits as well as the replacements have simple steel pins pressed into the top and bottom of the door and frame so it can be pivoted open or shut. Working brass hinges are also available in a range of styles, with small brass pins used to attach the hinges.

Do not attempt to pound the brass pins directly into the wood. Use a small awl, or hold one of the pins with a needlenose pliers and punch pilot holes for each of the pins. Tap the pins lightly into place with a hammer.

It takes a lot of patience to install two or three hinges so perfectly in line that the door will swing open smoothly. I suggest that you use brass hinges as "fakes." Use a razor saw to cut the pivoting portion from one half of each hinge, then nail the half with the pivot to the door and the other half to the wall. Install the hinges on the opening side of the door, but with the door closed. The hinges can be butted together so each looks like a working one.

Choose from a variety of door locks, door-face plates and doorknobs to finish the details. These can be obtained in just about every style. You'll find plastic replicas of glass knobs, with clear plastic in place of the glass. Address numbers in brass and mailboxes are also available to add final touches.

SCREEN DOORS

Yes, even miniature screen doors are available (but no storm doors or windows—yet). Laser Tech produces some incredibly intricate Victorian-era frames, but most dollhouse builders don't bother trying to simulate the screens. Dressmakers' tulle lace would be a fine choice if you want to create one yourself. Dye the lace black or gray and use a hot iron to press it perfectly flat. Use thick cyanoacrylate cement (Super Glue) to attach the tulle to one side of the door.

PAINTING WINDOWS AND DOORS

Thanks to some shortcuts, dollhouse windows and doors are easier to paint than their full-size counterparts. It is important to treat all the windows and doors as separate parts, painting them (and most of the trim) before they are installed.

Most nonworking windows are assembled

with one edge of the frame left loose so the clear plastic glazing can be removed while you paint. (See Fig. 7-6.) Remove the top, slide out the glazing and apply the paint. Use the same interior latex wall paints suggested for wood siding in Chapter 5. Buy the paint from a paint store; or, if you want smaller amounts, purchase the 8-ounce containers made by Borden's Builder's Choice (Accent Brand) from New England Hobby Supply, or Deco Art Americana from Dee's Delights.

On a real house, the windows, doors and trim are often painted with glossy or semi-gloss colors. To achieve that sheen on dollhouse doors and windows, spray the painted parts with clear acrylic enamel. Use semi-gloss, rather than gloss. Gloss paints often make the miniature parts so shiny they look like plastic. The window glazing must be protected with masking tape or removed because most clear spray paints will frost or etch the clear plastic.

FINISHING WITH A STAIN

You may want to stain the interior trim and, perhaps, some exterior doors and porch floors. In a Victorian house, you will probably want to stain the following items: floors, built-in cabinets, shutters, doors, interior doorjambs, thresholds, chair rails, wainscoting, staircases, banisters, baseboards, crown and corner mouldings, door blocks and any other wood.

Use an oil-based stain to minimize the chances of warping the thin wood pieces. Oil-based stains don't seem to raise the grain as much as water-based stains do. Apply the stain by dipping the parts in a shallow pan of stain, by wiping the stain onto the wood with a rag or by brushing it on.

Try a bit of the stain on a scrap of similar wood, perhaps on an area of an exterior frame you will later paint. Stains tend to look darker on dollhouses. The interior doors and window frames and trim will also be poorly illuminated. You'll probably discover that you want to thin the stain with an equal amount of thinner. Use the thinner suggested on the container. Allow 24 hours for the stain to dry completely.

When the stain is dry, sand it lightly with 220-grit sandpaper or, for an even smoother finish,

rub it with steel wool. Vacuum away any traces of dust and wipe the wood clean with a damp rag. Complete the finish with at least one coat of Deft Clear Wood Finish, Miniwax Semi-Gloss Polyurethane Varnish or a similar compound.

For the look of highly polished wood, apply another coat of clear finish and let it dry, then sand or rub the surface with steel wool and apply a third coat. Usually, three coats are enough. You can apply a coat of furniture paste wax, but most waxes tend to "yellow" and collect more dust than just the finished wood.

TIPS FOR PAINTING AND STAINING

The staining process will be much more enjoyable if you don't have to worry about your fingers and hands being brown for a month, so buy half a dozen pairs of disposable surgical gloves in a drugstore to protect your skin.

Also, use waxed paper to cover any areas where the parts will rest to dry. The parts won't stick to the waxed paper. Set the freshly painted or stained parts on the side that will be glued. Lean doors or windows against a heavy box (also covered with waxed paper) so only the very back edges of the frames contact the surface while the paint dries.

To minimize the chances of warping, always paint or stain both sides of any strips or thin panels. This is especially important with thin wood sheet material. The exceptions are wall panels, wainscoting, flooring or shingles that are glued down firmly with Quick Grab glue, as illustrated in Chapter 5.

PAINTING A WORKING WINDOW

Working windows usually have clear plastic glazing glued in place, and can only be painted in the same way that you would paint a real window. The tops of these windows are "free" so you can remove the panes. (See Fig. 7-7.) Then use a number 1–size brush to paint near the glazing and a ¼-inch brush to paint the remainder of the frame, but don't paint the edges of the sliding windows or the sliding tracks. (See Fig. 7-8 and Fig. 7-9 on page 70.)

I suggest that you use stain and not paint for the edges of sliding panes and their tracks. If

Fig. 7-8. Paint only the faces of the window panels, not the sliding edges.

Fig. 7-9. When painting the frames, keep the brush and paint away from the grooves where the panels slide.

7-10. Install the windows after both the exterior and interior are completely finished.

you prefer color, thin the acrylic paint with an equal part of water to make a colored stain. Use the edge of the brush to apply paint near the tracks and the edges. When the window paint has dried, inspect those areas and scrape away any paint that may have splashed onto them.

Use rubber cement to install the tops of any working windows and the windows themselves. The dried rubber cement is soft enough so it will tear easily. You can remove the window by prying lightly around its edges with a screwdriver.

If the working panes eventually stick, you can remove the window and the top to take out the sliding panes. Sand the edges of the panes to remove enough wood or paint so the panes will slide. Replace them in the frames, and then replace the top so you can glue the window back into the wall with rubber cement.

INSTALLING DOORS AND WINDOWS

By now you have tested each door and window to be certain it will fit, even with clapboard, brick or some other exterior finish. You have checked to see if the window needs to be shimmed with ⅛- or ¼-inch-square spacers so the interior trim will fit. You have also finished the wiring, painting and carpeting on the interior. Now you're ready to glue the window or door into its opening. (See Fig. 7-10).

The windows and doors can be held in place temporarily with a rolled-up inch of masking tape, sticky side out. Stick the tiny roll of tape on the upper edge of the window frame and push the window in place. In the photograph (See Fig. 7-11.), the Palladian-style double-casement window with the arched top is held in place with this method. The tape is just visible on the arch. It's easier to tell if a door or window is crooked when all the windows and doors are in place.

You may find that some of the openings are large enough to allow a window or door to tilt into a visibly crooked position. If the opening is

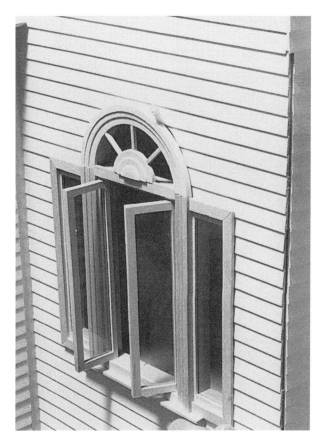

Fig. 7-11. Hold the windows in place temporarily with small rolls of masking tape.

oversize, insert a few toothpicks between the frame and the wall to force the door or window into the proper position.

From inside the dollhouse, look carefully at the window or door to see where it contacts the walls. Remove the window or door, then apply white glue or carpenter's glue to the contact areas and reinstall it.

CHAPTER EIGHT

PLAIN AND FANCY TRIM

Ask someone to describe a dollhouse, then a gingerbread house, and you'll probably get nearly identical answers. That's no wonder: Many miniature homes are adorned with that story-book-style trim. For a real-life, visual definition of a "gingerbread" house, look no further than the quaint Victorian row houses of San Francisco. That type of fancy trim—in fact, almost every type of fancy trim—is a standout feature on most finished dollhouses. (See Fig. 8-1.)

BASIC CORNER TRIM FOR KITS

Dollhouse kits have either wood or stucco exterior finishes, and each kit includes some type of trim for the outside corners. (The inside corners seldom have trim.) The die-cut ⅛-inch plywood houses have two wood strips that are to be joined to form an L-shaped corner moulding. The more expensive ¼- and ⅜-inch saw-cut plywood kits have milled-wood corners with angles already cut to fit the house.

I have found that it's best to save the corner trim for last. Install any trim on the top of the sides and around the foundation or basement, then install the corner trim. When you're ready for the corner trim, the following is the sequence I recommend.

Using the suggested sequence for assembly in the kit's instructions, test-fit each piece of trim before painting the pieces or gluing them in place. Hold the trim temporarily in place with masking tape. If you find any pieces that are either too short or too long, you have probably used a wrong piece somewhere on the house.

Paint all the trim pieces before gluing them

to the dollhouse. (See Fig. 8-2 on page 74.) Test-fit all the painted pieces again, and lay them on the workshop floor near their locations so you can position them properly on the finished house. (See Fig. 8-3 on page 74.) Use white glue or carpenter's glue to install the trim. Hold it in place with two pieces of masking tape while the glue dries.

FITTING CORNER TRIM TO CUSTOM SHELLS

One purpose for corner trim is to hide the rough ends of clapboard or other wood siding. On real homes, it also protects the exposed end grain on

Fig. 8-1. Roy Davis customized this Real Good Toys' "Woodstock" with the optional gazebo-style wrap-around porch. The windows are all custom replacements from Houseworks.

Fig. 8-2. Paint all the trim before installing it on the dollhouse.

Fig. 8-3. Test-fit the trim to be sure it's going in the right place. Here, the porch roof will be installed below the trim.

the clapboards from the weather. Trim is a gift to the inexperienced carpenter; it can cover up minor cutting errors, glue smears and other mistakes.

Northeastern Scale Models, Houseworks, Handley House and others offer milled-wood angles in ⅜- and ½-inch widths. The ⅜-inch angle produces a much finer finished appearance on most dollhouses. The ½-inch angle looks best on the corners of Tudor-style dollhouses.

Buy a small modeler's miter box at a dollhouse or hobby store, and get a razor saw with a blade to match the depth of the notches in the miter box. Measure the length needed for any one of the corner trim pieces, mark it on the wooden angle and cut at that mark in the miter box. In Chapter 14 there is an illustration of the miter box in use.

Trim for inside corners is optional. Usually, the clapboard sheathing or bricks can be fitted to overlap each other nicely at the inside corners. Any lack of a precise fit can be moved to the outside corners and covered with trim. If you want to apply trim to the inside corners, use the same ⅜-inch angle-shaped milled-wood pieces, but turn them around so they are attached on their outside faces.

TRIM FOR HINGED WALLS

Many dollhouse kits have at least one hinged front wall; some, called "front opening" doll-

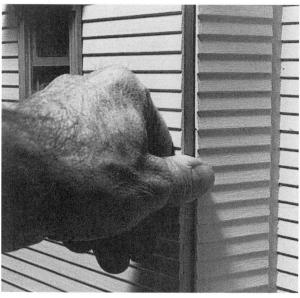

Fig. 8-4. Add a shim to the edge of opening front panels, allowing the corner trim to hide the seam.

houses, have the entire front wall hinged. If you want to customize such a dollhouse, use the long piano hinges made by Northeastern. They're available through most dollhouse shops. The outside corner trim can be used to disguise the corners of these hinged walls.

Both of the corners must be in exact alignment with each other, with no gaps. If necessary, add a shim like the piece of ¹⁄₁₆ x ⅛-inch wood on the hinged wall. (See Fig. 8-4.) The ⅜-inch wood angle trim furnished with a Real Good Toys kit

Fig. 8-5. Laser Tech trim has been used to customize this "Noel Thomas Tower House."

will now cover the right edge of the front wall and will overlap ⅛ inch onto the adjoining wall.

If you apply a ⅜-inch angle to the left wall, it will interfere with the working of the hinges. Tape the wood angle in place and mark the flange that is going to fit against the adjacent wall. Sand about ⅛ inch from that flange. Remove just enough wood so the angle will cover only the front wall's clapboard siding and the thickness of the plywood wall. Tape the angle onto the corner and test the operation of the hinged wall. The wall should open effectively with the angle in place.

CHAIR RAIL TRIM

Some Victorian houses had exterior decorative horizontal trim, sometimes set at the level of the window sills like interior wainscoting. On most Victorians, however, the trim seems to have been placed at random. To see if that look would suit your dollhouse, refer to one of the dozens of books that reproduce original drawings of Victorian homes. You might also study the illustrations of several books that depict San Francisco's famous Victorian townhouses.

"Noel Thomas Tower House," an Evergreen Woodworker shell finished by Norm Nielsen, is a particularly fine example of the use of chair rail trim and other Victorian architectural design features. (See Fig. 8-5.) Northeastern, Miniature House and Real Life Products offer milled-wood chair rails. Chair rail trim has also been applied to eaves of Norm's Dollhouse's "Georgetown," finished by David Nielsen. These houses are shown on the cover and in the color section.

A lone chair rail runs all around the "Noel Thomas Tower House," starting above the inset corner windows on the chimney wall. Another, topped by vertical pieces of Northeastern milled-wood bead and board–style siding, is placed

Fig. 8-6. This is the scroll saw-style trim supplied with some Real Good Toys dollhouse kits.

around the tower just below the windows. Triangles of siding are also placed above a chair rail beneath the eaves. The exterior walls are finished with horizontal Northeastern Novelty-style siding.

Accents like these add an incredibly authentic appearance to a gingerbread dollhouse. Once again, these pieces should be carefully fitted, then removed and painted, before being installed. Paint the back and front of the chair rail to seal the gluing face and prevent warping. Use Quick Grab Cement by 3C to install the strips.

TRIM FOR EAVES AND APEXES

Most kits include both finishing trim and ornate gingerbread-style decorative trim to fit along the sloping side edges of the roof (the eaves) and beneath the peaked ends (the apexes). (See Fig. 8-6.)

The ends of the roof's boards, on both real and miniature houses, are protected by trim. On contemporary homes, it may be just 1 x 4 boards. On houses built in the first half of the 1900s, the boards are more likely to be of the milled-wood type with several ornate internal and external curves and angles.

The better-quality kits include the ornate trim boards for the ends of the roof. Inexpensive die-cut kits usually include a simple board or a piece of gingerbread trim, which serves as both the board and the decorative trim. Several styles are available from Northeastern and Miniature House to upgrade any of the kits.

TRIM FOR HORIZONTAL EAVES

Some type of trim for the horizontal eaves at the bottom edges of the roof panels is also included in better-quality kits. (See Fig. 8-7.) Again, this trim is designed to protect the ends of the roof boards. On real homes, it usually overhangs slightly downward to keep rain from running up beneath the roof. Most kits include a $\frac{1}{16}$ x $\frac{1}{4}$-inch (1 x 4, in dollhouse scale) piece for each of these lower edges. This board will serve as the mounting place for any rain gutters you might choose to add.

When installing ornate milled-wood trim around the eaves, you may want to cut 45-degree miters for the corner joints. The miter box and a razor saw shown in Chapter 14 will help make the cut a true 45-degree angle. The final joint will have to be sanded to fit properly.

GINGERBREAD TRIM FOR EAVES AND APEXES

Ornate gingerbread trim, included even in inexpensive kits, can be installed behind the simple trim boards. Each roof requires at least three pieces of this trim: the triangular apex and two long, thin pieces to fit along each of the roof's sloping edges. Several styles of apex trim are available, and there are dozens of different styles of ornate trim for the eaves. You can add these pieces to farmhouse-style kits to help create a Victorian appearance.

To install the gingerbread trim, start with the apex. Most likely, you will have to cut a little from each side of the trim to match its angle to that of the roof. Depending on the trim, it may be best to cut the apex piece in half vertically, then remove the material from the middle to adjust the angle. The two halves can be joined by a piece of $\frac{1}{16}$-inch-square wood like that shown on the "Noel Thomas Tower

Fig. 8-7. *Install a piece of facia trim along the horizontal eves of the roof.*

House." Cement the ornate trim beneath the standard roof trim with a quick-setting sticky cement such as Tacky Glue or Quick Grab.

Cut the longer pieces of gingerbread trim to fit the remaining length of the edges. Look at photographs of real Victorian houses to see how the bottom edges of both the roof trim and gingerbread trim are cut and beveled. Again, the trim on the "Noel Thomas Tower House" can serve as a guide. The roof trim on most real Victorian houses was extremely ornate, and until recently it's been impossible to recreate those fancy cut-out holes, slots and curves with steel dies. Fortunately, several manufacturers, including Northeastern and Laser Tech, have introduced incredibly ornate apex and eave trim and roof ridge mouldings, which are cut from trim sheets of wood. The trim is relatively expensive, but it lends a light, realistic look to any Victorian-era dollhouse.

GINGERBREAD TRIM FOR ROOF RIDGES

The peak or ridge of the roof should be finished with some type of flashing or shingles. Triangular-shaped milled-wood strips are available that will both finish the ridge and provide a mounting channel to accept your choice of the gingerbread ridge trim. Install the ornate trim after the shingles and ridge trim are in place.

Some of those triangular strips, including Houseworks' 7060, 7061 and 7062, are designed to duplicate the stamped-metal roof ridge trim on real houses. These mouldings are supposed to simulate steel, so take special care to seal, paint and sand the finish to produce a smooth and shiny surface.

On some of the less expensive dollhouses, the ridge trim serves both as a finishing piece for the ridge and as decorative trim. That certainly

Fig. 8-8. The soffit on this "Noel Thomas Tower House" has been embellished with Northeastern Scale Models laser-cut gingerbread.

makes it quicker and easier to finish off the roof ridge, but it doesn't match the appearance of a real house. Still, you may decide that the trim by itself is enough to finish the ridge on your doll-house.

GINGERBREAD TRIM FOR BAY WINDOWS AND SOFFITS

Assembled bay windows are available from most of the firms that make regular windows. On a Victorian house, the bottom of the bay window might be embellished with brackets and perhaps a ball.

The overhanging soffit was also a common architectural detail on full-size Victorian houses. There are two of them on the "Noel Thomas Tower House." (See Fig. 8-8.) This detail can be added to many Victorian dollhouse kits or shells,

but it would have to be done when the shell was being assembled. Presently, there are no kits available that reproduce this architectural feature, but you can fashion your own.

Trim a soffit or the bottom of a bay window with one of the ornate "corbel brackets" (such as Houseworks' 7026) or an "eaves bracket" (such as Houseworks 7027 or 7028, or Northeastern's 1221—shown on the "Noel Thomas Tower House"). For the balls, cut the small ones from the tops of staircase posts.

PAINTING EXTERIOR TRIM

It shouldn't take more than a coat or two of paint to hide most of the fine grain of milled and laser-cut trim. Art Deco Americana, Builder's Choice and Borden's Accent 8-ounce jars of interior latex wall paint are ideal for painting trim.

Fig. 8-9. Paint the trim before installing the shingles.

It may be easier to paint the milled-wood trim for the eaves after it has been glued to the edges of the roof. Paint the gingerbread trim as separate pieces in a contrasting color. Be sure to paint both sides so the wood doesn't warp. (See Fig. 8-9.)

The trim is easiest to paint if you use a brush that's about the width of the trim. (See Fig. 8-10.) Wear disposable surgical gloves as you work. Lay both the pre-fitted and cut strips on a large piece of waxed paper. Brush the paint onto two sides of the trim and let it dry. Flip the trim over (180 degrees) and paint the remaining sides.

When the paint dries, smooth the surfaces to remove any splinters or wisps of wood. Hold a piece of steel wool in your hand and gently pull each piece of trim through the steel wool. This is a lot quicker than trying to force sandpaper into all the intricate curves and hollows. See Chapter 7 for additional painting tips.

Many dollhouse builders feel that trim looks most realistic if it has a bit more gloss or shine than the walls. To achieve that look, spray the painted trim with clear acrylic semi-gloss paint; gloss paints sometimes make the parts look like plastic.

RAIN GUTTERS AND DOWNSPOUTS

For additional realism, why not give your dollhouse rain gutters and downspouts? Northeastern makes a milled-wood rain gutter in 22-inch lengths. Cut pieces to fit against the horizontal eaves of the roof, and glue a scrap of a business card (it's the right thickness) to the open ends. When the glue dries, use a hobby knife to slice the edges of the card to match the shape of the rain gutter. Paint the gutter when you paint the trim.

Study real houses to see where rain gutters

Fig. 8-10. For the easiest to paint job, choose a brush that's nearly the same width as the trim.

are located. You'll notice that they have a slight pitch. This is an important detail. If done carefully on the dollhouse, you'll get the right effect. But if the angle is too pronounced, it will make the roof look crooked. Use Tacky Glue to install the gutters.

Now, look at real houses to see where the downspouts are located. You can simulate a downspout with a ⅛-inch-diameter dowel. Use the miter box and razor saw to make 45-degree cuts through the dowel. Rotate the cut part of the dowel about 120 degrees and glue it back together to make the angle near the bottom open end on most downspouts. For a fine detail, make two cuts, about a half-inch apart, near the top of the downspout so it can reach from the side of the house out to the gutter on the eave of the roof. The photograph shows a downspout added to one of Duracraft's "Lafayette" dollhouses. (See Fig. 8-11.)

An alternative method of duplicating a downspout is to use K & S or similar-brand ⅛-inch-diameter aluminum tubing. Use pliers to make gentle bends in the tube (if you bend it too sharply, it will crimp). Cut the tube with a razor saw and use a flat file to remove any burrs. (See Fig. 8-12.) The techniques described for the ⅛-inch wood dowel can be used to cut the aluminum tube. Assemble the cut parts with five-minute epoxy; when that dries, file the joints to a smooth radius.

Paint the downspout to match the nearest trim. Paint ⅛-inch cubes of wood to match the wall and glue them to the wall immediately behind the downspout. Then glue the downspout to the cubes to space it away from the wall. (See Fig. 8-13.)

Fig. 8-11. A downspout can be made from a wood dowel.

Fig. 8-13. Place the downspouts in the same positions that you'd find them on a real house.

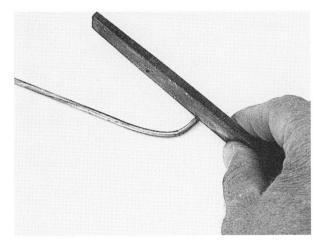

Fig. 8-12. File the cut end of a downspout made from aluminum tube.

CHAPTER NINE

SHINGLE, TILE AND METAL ROOFING

You can top off your dollhouse with almost any kind of roofing material: wood, asphalt or slate shingles, shakes, tiles or corrugated metal or copper. With the exception of imitation slate and corrugated aluminum (in place of steel), all of these shingles and roofing materials are made of the same materials you'd find on a real house. Fortunately, it's fun—not work—to install the roof on a dollhouse.

PLASTIC ROOFING SHEETS

If you're in a hurry, try the solid sheets of vacuum-formed plastic roofing materials. Fancy shingles as well as those made of wood, asphalt, slate and corrugated metal are sold by Precision

Products. Wood and shake shingles, Spanish tile and round-edge roof tiles are available from Plastruct. Most of those panels are unpainted, although Miniature House, Plastruct and JR Enterprises offer colored Spanish tile roofs in this form.

PAINTING THE SHINGLES AND TILES

It's easiest to paint the sheets before cutting them apart. Latex interior wall paints can be used for colored shingles. For wooden shingles, start with a light yellow-beige about the color of pine. Brush the paint over the entire sheet, and let it dry.

Mix a "wash" of four parts water to one part dark brown (burnt umber) latex or acrylic paint. Hold the sheet with the area that will end up near the peak of the roof at the bottom. Brush this dark brown wash over the roof. (See Fig. 9-1.)

The diluted brown color should run down the sheet and accumulate in the edges, creating "shadows" between horizontal rows of shingles and accenting the simulated grain of wooden shingles. Let the paint dry before you judge the results. If you don't get the desired effect, experiment with the mixture of water and paint. If the wash is simply imparting an even brown color to the roof, try adding a bit more water. If all the brown is puddling along the horizontal rows, add more paint.

INSTALLING THE SHINGLES AND TILES

This roofing material is the same as the vacuumed-formed brick and stone sheets for walls or

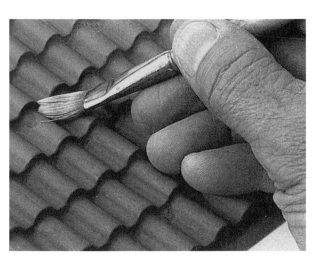

Fig. 9-1. Coat the vacuum-formed tile or shingle roofs with a wash of dark brown paint.

Fig. 9-2. Use a hobby knife to cut the edges of the vacuum-formed plastic sheets of shingles.

Fig. 9-3. Fit the vacuum-formed shingles carefully and no metal flashing or moulding cover will be needed.

Fig. 9-4. The Precision Products vacuum-formed shingle sheets include these special ridge pieces.

Fig. 9-5. Smooth plastic, cut from the edges of the shingle sheets, can be used as flashing.

floors discussed in Chapter 6. To install the sheets, start with the largest areas of the roof so the leftovers can be used for smaller areas. Hold the sheet over the roof and mark the edges of the roof on the back of the sheet. Use scissors to cut the sheet to size.

If the roof area is larger than the width of the plastic sheet, cut the unfinished edge from both sides of the first sheet. Lay it in place on the roof. Use a hobby knife to cut around the edges of individual shingles on the adjoining edge of

the second sheet. (See Fig. 9-2.) Produce a "missing tooth" pattern in the rows of shingles. Let this panel lay over the top of the first panel by about ¼ inch. Continue overlapping panels until the shingles run across the roof.

Use a similar technique to overlap two or more sheets of plastic shingles going up the slope of the roof. Start with the sheet along the bottom eaves. Cut the next sheet along the lower edge, following the pattern of the shingles. Let that cut edge lay over the top of the first

Fig. 9-6. Real wood shingles are available to duplicate several patterns, including this octagon butt pattern.

½-inch piece of copper foil in half and cement it to the ridge. Another option is to cut smooth plastic from the edges of the shingle sheets and use it for flashing. (See Fig. 9-5.) For Spanish tiles, merely cut a single long vertical row of tiles from the sheet and glue it across the ridge (so the ridge tiles run 90 degrees to the regular ones). Cement the ridge pieces to the roof with clear silicone bathtub caulking compound.

REAL WOOD SHINGLES

There's a wide selection of individual real wood shingles available for dollhouses. You'll find them with tapers, like shakes, and as straight wood, like common shingles. There's also a choice of flat, rounded and rectangular ends to produce square butt, octagon butt, fishtail, diamond, handsplit hexagon and handsplit fishtail patterns. (See Fig. 9-6.) Miniature Manors makes some unusual shingles that produce curved, inverted fish scale, large octagon, beaded, rounded-square or heart-shaped patterns. Most of these shingles are offered in either basswood or cedar.

The finished roof's appearance will depend a lot on how carefully you install the shingles. The shake look is the easiest to reproduce because you needn't be extremely accurate with installation. Duplicating the trim and even the appearance of real wood conventional shingles requires much more patience and care.

Preparation is extremely important when installing individual shingles. First, paint the roof a color close to its finished shade. Next, decide if you want to stain the shingles or paint them. Of course, the shingles can be left unpainted to look like a house that has just been fitted with fresh wood shingles.

sheet. Repeat the process again, if necessary. (See Fig. 9-3.) When the roof is covered, mark the ridge line and cut the top sheet along that line.

When all the roof panels are cut to size, glue them in place with clear silicone bathtub caulking compound or double-sided carpet tape, as described in Chapter 6. Touch up the stark white cut edges with a dark brown felt-tip pen.

FINISHING THE ROOF RIDGES

Many sheets include special pieces for trim at the ridges and flashing in the inside corners. (See Fig. 9-4.) You could also use one of the Houseworks milled-wood ridge pieces, or fold a

STAINING SHINGLES

Measure the total number of square inches on the roof. The packages of shingles list how many square inches they'll cover, so buy enough to meet your needs.

Use an oil-based stain to minimize warping. Fill a shallow pie pan with the stain and, wearing disposable rubber gloves, drop in enough shingles to cover the bottom with a single layer.

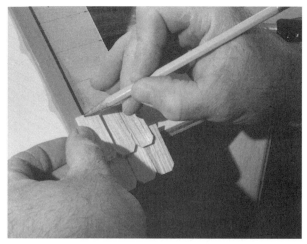

Fig. 9-7. Mark the location for the top of the first row of wood shingles.

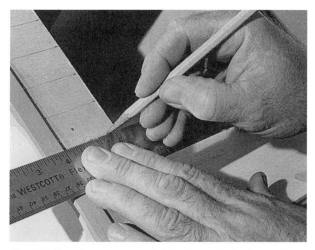

Fig. 9-8. Test-fit two rows of shingles to help determine the proper vertical spacing.

Fig. 9-9. Apply a bead of Tacky glue to the roof and another to the upper edges of the shingles.

Remove the shingles and place them to dry on a piece of waxed paper. Repeat the process until you have stained enough shingles to cover the entire roof.

If you want to simulate a weathered shake roof, use a light gray stain. Experiment on a few shingles to determine the proper amount of color. Lay the shingles out on waxed paper and use a paintbrush to cover one side with stain. Painting just one side should force the shingles to warp like real weather-worn shakes. For greater warping effect, try one of the water-based stains.

INSTALLING THE SHINGLES

Start with the largest area of the roof. Decide if you want the shingles to just reach the lower edge of the roof (or the rain gutter) or to hang over it by ⅛ inch. Mark the location for the top of the first row of wood shingles. (See Fig. 9-7.) Use masking tape to hold the first shingle in place along the lower edge.

Hold the next shingle up the roof, overlapping the first. Move it up or down until you have exposed the desired amount of the first shingle. Make a pencil mark on the roof where the top of the second shingle rests. Measure the distance between the top of the first shingle and your mark. That is the vertical spacing for all the shingles on all areas the roof. (See Fig. 9-8.) Make marks to match that vertical spacing all the way up the roof. When you reach the ridge, you'll likely find there isn't quite enough room to make a full-width "exposed shingle" mark. The top row needs to be wide enough to include the exposed-shingle dimension plus ¼ inch to leave room for the ridge covering. Make a mark to match that total space down the roof from the ridge.

Divide the "missing" room for the last top row by the number of rows of shingles, and adjust the size of your exposed-shingle dimension by that amount. Make new pencil marks up the roof, each spaced to that new exposed-shin-

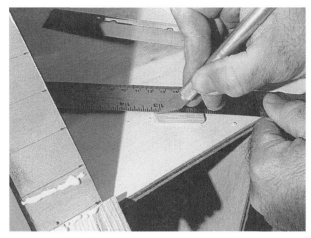

Fig. 9-10. Start the next row of shingles with a half-shingle. Cut it with a knife or a razor saw.

Fig. 9-11. Sand the cut edge of the shingle on a sanding block.

Fig. 9-12. It's not necessary to cut all the way through the shingle. Simply slice lightly, then break the shingle along the cut.

gle dimension, and do the the same on the opposite edge of the roof. Connect the marks with pencil lines all the way across the roof.

If you'll be painting or staining the shingles after they're glued to the roof, use the same Quick Grab Cement by 3C that you did to install the clapboard wall trim. (See Chapter 5.) If you have prestained the shingles or you're not going to paint them, use a Tacky type of glue that becomes sticky almost immediately.

Run a bead of the cement about 12 inches

along the bottom edge of the roof. (See Fig. 9-9.) Start the row with a whole shingle, adding a shingle at a time until you reach the other side. Butt the top of each shingle against the first pencil line. If the roof is wider than 12 inches, apply more glue. In the photos, I'm working on a 2-inch-wide section of the open side of the roof.

When you reach the other side of the roof, mark a cutting line on the underside of the last shingle, which should fit right up to the roof's edge. Use a razor saw to cut it to the correct width. (See Fig. 9-10.) Sand the cut edge. (See Fig. 9-11.) Place the shingle at the edge of the roof, or do as some builders prefer—remove the next-to-last shingle and place the shortened shingle in one row from the edge.

For the second row, cut one shingle exactly in half. It's not necessary to cut completely through the shingle. Just slice lightly and break the shingle along the cut. (See Fig. 9-12 on this page and Fig. 9-13 on page 88.) Go back to the starting edge. Run the bead of glue a foot along the roof just below the pencil line. That's the place where the shingles will rest. Run a second bead of glue along the top edge of the first row of shingles. Start laying the second row with the half shingle. (See Fig. 9-14 on page 88.) Keep adding full shingles until you reach the opposite end, pressing each shingle tightly against the adjacent shingle. (See Fig. 9-15 on page 88.) Mark and cut the last shingle to fit. The excess

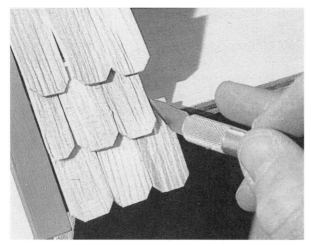

Fig. 9-13. Cut the excess shingles cut after all the rows are in place.

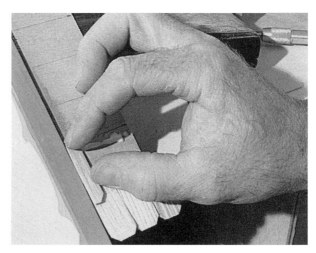

Fig. 9-14. Glue the half-shingle to the outer edge of the roof to start the second row of shingles.

Fig. 9-15. Press each shingle tightly against the adjacent shingle.

Fig. 9-16. Use a razor saw to cut each of the shingles on the top row to the same length.

shingles can be trimmed after all the rows are in place.

Repeat the process a row at a time, starting every other row with a half-shingle. When you get to the top row, each shingle must be trimmed to match the exposed-shingle dimension plus about ¼ inch for covering the ridge. Cut the shingles with a razor saw, then apply the

glue and lay the final row. (See Fig. 9-16.) Repeat this process for each of the roof panels.

FINISHING THE RIDGE

There are several methods for finishing the ridge on a shingled roof: Individual shingles can be cut in half and run across the ridge, or it can be covered with a ½-inch piece of copper foil, folded down the center and glued in place with silicone bathtub caulking compound. You can cover the ridge with one of the milled-wood ridge pieces from Houseworks or with two pieces of ¹⁄₁₆ x ⅜-inch wood, joined to make an angle. The wood ridge angle can be stained or painted to match the shingles or painted a contrasting color.

The inside corners, where dormers or gables join the main roof, can be covered with shingles cut to fit the corner and left as is. That area can also be covered with a copper flashing. Cut a ½-inch-wide piece of copper foil, crease it down the middle and attach it with clear silicone bathtub caulking compound.

ASPHALT SHINGLES

Genuine asphalt shingles are available from What's Next?, ganged as single rows in strips 1 foot or 3 feet long. Use the same procedure described for wooden shingles to mark the roof and cut the shingles. Tacky glue should be strong enough to hold the asphalt shingles. You can lay an entire row at a time. Trim off the odd shingle at the end of each row, and cut off a half shingle at the start of every other row. Finish the ridges and inner corners as described for wooden shingles.

For an alternative ridge treatment with asphalt shingles, cut one of the sheets of plain asphalt roofing into a ½-inch strip. Fold the strip in half and cement it across the ridge with clear silicone bathtub caulking compound.

CORRUGATED METAL ROOFING

Handley House has 12 x 12-inch sheets of aluminum formed to match l/12-scale corrugated steel. (Real corrugated roofing is usually sold in sheets that are 6 or 8 feet long.) Cut across the middle of the sheet to produce two rows of corrugated metal, each being 6 feet wide to scale. Miniature House has 8 x 4-inch sheets of vacuum-formed plastic that's painted silver to simulate galvanized corrugated iron.

Use the techniques described earlier for sheet plastic roof finishes to install the corrugated metal. Start with the sheet nearest the lower edge of the roof. Add the second sheet, overlapping the first by about ⅛ inch. If the roof is tall enough, add another sheet, overlapping the second sheet. When the sheets reach the ridge, mark the ridge across the back of the sheet and cut the sheet along that mark. Finish the ridge with one of the Houseworks 7060, 7061 or 7062 simulated-metal milled-wood ridge pieces.

SHEET ASPHALT ROOFS

What's Next? also makes genuine sheet asphalt roofing in 6 x 24-inch pieces. There is a choice of black or 10 other colors. On real roofs, the asphalt is usually applied in 4-foot rolls which run across the roof. Cut the What's Next? asphalt into 4-inch wide strips, and apply them to the roof, starting at the bottom. Overlap the first piece by about ⅛ inch. Finish the ridge with the Houseworks 7060, 7061 or 7062 molded-wood replica of metal roof ridge pieces. The ridge can also be covered with two pieces of ¹⁄₁₆ x ⅜-inch wood, joined to make an angle and painted to match the trim—a far more likely treatment for such an inexpensive roof.

SHEET METAL ROOFS

Usually, real roofs covered with sheet metal have horizontal seams about every 2 feet. Simulate those seams by gluing ¹⁄₁₆-inch-square strips of wood directly to the roof. If the roof span is not divisible by 2, fit the shortest span on one end of the roof. No wood strips are needed at the edges. Coat the entire roof with clear silicone bathtub caulking compound, and cover it with heavy-duty household aluminum foil. Use the Houseworks 7060, 70061 or 7061 milled-wood ridge pieces. Finally, paint the roof silver. When the paint dries, spray the roof with Testor's Dullcote to give it the gray look of weathered tin.

If you want to simulate a copper-covered roof on a Victorian house, use the same technique, but cover the roof with Dee's Delights' Copper Foil. Since copper roofs oxidize to a dull lime green, another method is to cover the roof with aluminum foil and paint it a dull green.

Fig. 10-1. The plywood shell is the same on several Real Good Toys dollhouses. This 700D kit has been customized with a full-width porch kit. **Photo courtesy Real Good Toys.**

Fig. 10-2. The Real Good Toys 700D dollhouse here has an additional room and a wraparound gazebo porch from a kit. **Photo courtesy Real Good Toys.**

Fig. 10-3. Here a two-story "Plantation" porch has been added to a Real Good Toys 700D dollhouse. **Photo courtesy Real Good Toys.**

Fig. 10-4. A "Plantation" porch and two side rooms have been added to this Real Good Toys 700D dollhouse for still another look. **Photo courtesy Real Good Toys.**

CHAPTER TEN

PORCHES, CHIMNEYS AND GARAGES

A front porch or patio can alter the appearance of a dollhouse more effectively than any other single architectural element. The porch, in fact, is often the one detail that makes even a less expensive shell look like a costly custom dollhouse. (See Fig. 10-1, Fig. 10-2 and Fig. 10-3.)

Other exterior additions such as left and right extensions can also change the look of a dollhouse. (See Fig. 10-4, Fig. 10-5 and Fig. 10-6) An often-overlooked detail is a chimney, which can be added, in minute detail, to any dollhouse kit. You can also fashion a simple garage or build one from a kit.

ADDING A PORCH

The porch itself is such a fascinating dollhouse project that Houseworks and others offer simple porch shell kits. These include nothing but two walls with a door and two precut window openings, a floor and a roof. It's up to you to finish the shell and to decorate it appropriately, using the same techniques you'd use to finish a whole house. You'll find porch swings, hanging plants, planters and kids' toys—just about anything you can imagine on a real porch—at dollhouse shops.

The porch kit makes an interesting project for those who want to learn how to finish a doll-

Fig. 10-5. Right and left extensions give this basic 700D Real Good Toys dollhouse a much different appearance. **Photo courtesy Real Good Toys.**

Fig. 10-6. Extensions plus a porch give yet another appearance to the basic 700D Real Good Toys dollhouse. **Photo courtesy Real Good Toys.**

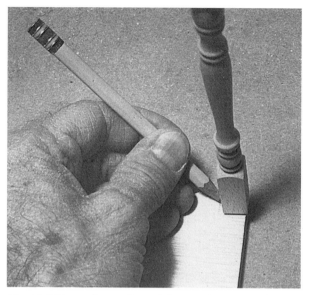

Fig. 10-7. Trace the outline of the porch post on the porch floor.

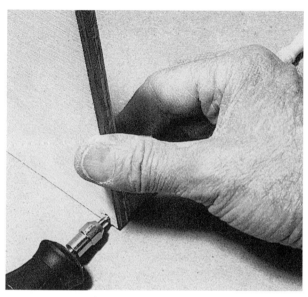

Fig. 10-8. Drill a ³⁄₃₂-inch hole through the porch and into the bottom of the porch post.

Fig. 10-9. Check the fit of the ³⁄₃₂-inch dowel in the drilled hole.

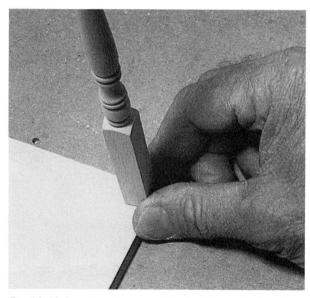

Fig. 10-10. Insert and cement the post into the hole in the porch.

house but lack the space for an entire house. The kits are available in both l/12-scale and half-scale. Houseworks has a booklet, *Porches Across America*, that includes full-size templates for people who would prefer to cut out their own porch shell from ³⁄₈-inch plywood, plus instructions and photos for making 13 different porch scenes.

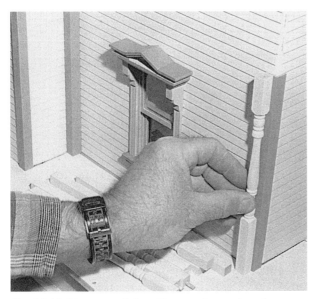

Fig. 10-11. Use one of the pillars to determine the length of the trim under the roof.

Fig. 10-12. Use a 3/8-inch square post to support the porch roof.

ASSEMBLING THE PILLARS

In most kits, tall columns or pillars made of turned wood (some dollhouse makers call them spindles) support the porches. The instructions suggest that these posts can be glued to the porch floor. For greater strength, however, it's better to install a ³⁄₃₂-inch dowel in the bottom of each post. The dowel will help keep the post in alignment even if one of the glue joints breaks.

Install any wood deck or simulated stone or brick surface on the porch. Set each pillar in the proper position. Usually, the railings define the pillar locations because they must fit tightly between the pillars. Temporarily place all the railings on the floor of the porch, with each between the proper pair of pillars. Use a pencil to mark the position of each pillar on the porch floor. (See Fig. 10-7.) Also, trace the square outline of the base of each pillar onto the floor.

Use an electric drill or a motor tool to drill a ³⁄₃₂-inch hole half an inch deep into the center of the bottom of each pillar. (See Fig. 10-8.) Drill a matching ³⁄₃₂-inch hole in the exact center of the pencil-marked square of the floor. For a loose fit, wiggle the drill slightly in the holes.

Cut a ³⁄₃₂-inch dowel 1 inch long for each pillar. Press the dowels into the bottoms of the pil-

lars. (See Fig. 10-9.) Do not glue any of the dowels or pillars in place until all of the railings are finished and glued to the pillars. You may need to enlarge one or more of the holes in the floor to make everything fit properly. When the railings are installed, insert and cement the pillars into the holes. (See Fig. 10-10.)

ASSEMBLING THE ROOF

With most add-on porch kits, the corner trim must be cut to clear the supports for the roof. Use one of the pillars to determine the length of the trim below the roof. (See Fig. 10-11.) The trim on the top must be cut at an angle to match that of the roof after the porch has been assembled. The length of each piece of corner trim will be shorter by the thickness of the porch roof, and the trim will now be in two pieces.

The Real Good Toys porch kit includes pre-cut pieces of trim as well as ⅜-inch-square pieces of wood for the inside corners of the dollhouse walls. If you are building your own porch roof, you will want to cut some ⅜-inch-square roof-support posts to match the length of those pillars. (See Fig. 10-12.)

Paint the revised trim and the posts and let the paint dry. Hold the posts and trim in place

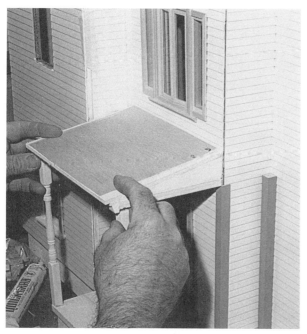

Fig. 10-13. Install the porch one section at a time, beginning with the section over the front door.

Fig. 10-14. The gazebo roof in the Real Good Toys porch kit fits perfectly against the adjacent porch roof panels.

Fig. 10-15. Roy Davis has installed the wraparound gazebo porch, which is ready for installation of the railings.

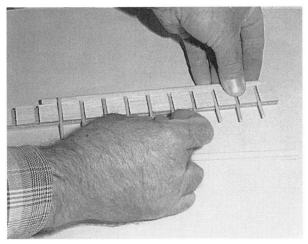

Fig. 10-16. Place a porch railing post into each of the slots in the assembly jig.

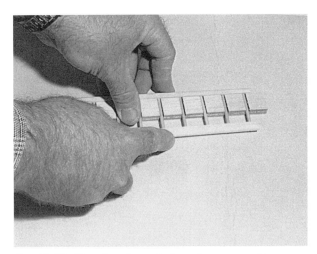

Fig. 10-17. Glue the channel-shaped upper and lower porch railings to the ends of the porch posts.

with masking tape or a dab of sticky wax like Mini-Hold, from Dee's Delights, or Hold, from the Miniature Lumber Shoppe. Assemble the roof pieces and hold them in place on the pillars and trim. Test-fit all of the pieces. (See Fig. 10-13, Fig. 10-14 and Fig. 10-15.) If the fit is satisfactory, paint the roof trim. Do not glue the posts, pillars and roof together until all of the painting has been completed and the floor foundation of the porch has been finished.

PAINTING THE RAILINGS AND POSTS

Some dollhouse kits as well as several porch kits include porch railings. Real Good Toys includes a simple milled-wood jig to assemble the railings, and the dowel posts are all precut.

Paint the railings and posts before assembly. It's wise to paint all the components separately so you can use more than one color. Often, several bands of colors encircled Victorian pillars and railing posts. To get that look on a model, begin by painting the pillars and posts with their major color. Apply the usual two coats, sanding after the first coat to smooth the surface.

Next, find a small cardboard box (for a jig) that's a bit shorter than the pillars and another small box (for a jig) that's a bit shorter than the posts. Cut numerous equally spaced notches along both sides of the boxes so several posts or

pillars can lay crosswise in the notches at once. Turn each pillar or post with one hand, while you apply a thin line of paint with the other hand. This method ("the jig") also works well for painting stair railing posts.

ASSEMBLING THE RAILING

To assemble a railing, place a post in each of the notches of the jig until you have enough to fit the length of railing. (See Fig. 10-16.) Next, fill one of the wood channels of the railing with white glue and press the railing over the top of the row of posts.

Fill the bottom porch railing channel with white glue and push it onto the bottom of the row of posts. (See Fig. 10-17.) Be sure that the row of posts is centered in the two channels. Gently lift the assembled railing from the jig and set the railing on a piece of waxed paper until the glue dries.

You can create much more ornate railings from milled-wood parts. Use two 12-inch-long scraps of ½ x 1-inch wood to make a jig for assembling your own porch railing. Cut spacer blocks from the first piece to match the distance you want between the posts. If that distance is ¼ inch, then cut about 40 of the ¼-inch blocks. At the width of a post apart, cement them along the second ½ x 1 piece to build a notched jig

Fig. 10-18. Northeastern Scale Models' posts and laser-cut gingerbread were used to customize the porch on the "Noel Thomas Tower House."

that resembles the one furnished with the Real Good Toys porch kits. Let the glue dry, and use the jig as described earlier.

Most add-on porch kits include railings and steps. The railings, however, are simple wood channels with uniformly round wood dowels for the posts. For ornate Victorian-style components, including railings and a variety of turned posts as well as roof-height pillars, Northeastern and Laser Tech have a number of laser-cut parts that simulate scroll saw-cut Victorian porch railing faces. (See Fig. 10-18.) These can be used with the upper and lower railings from porch kits or with the more ornate railings.

Some Victorian porches had foot-wide railings suspended near the ceiling, with the scroll saw-cut gingerbread in these areas. These, too, are available for dollhouses as preassembled or laser-cut pieces.

ADDING THE FLOOR AND FOUNDATION

The array of porch floors you'll find in the real world can be duplicated in miniature. Wood flooring, including special patterns for porches, is an obvious choice. Imitation slate is also available; Dee's Delights' Mini-Slat simulates random patterns. Ready-to-lay square slates with grouting are available from Lawbre and others.

The face or foundation of the porch can be modeled in brick or stone, using the techniques described in Chapter 6. (See Fig. 10-19.) Many Victorian-era porches, however, were faced in wood latticework with diamond-shaped openings. Miniature House makes that lattice in 1½ x 12-inch pieces; Miniature Lumber Shoppe has it in 2 x 12- and 2 x 24-inch pieces; Timberbrook, in 2 x 8-inch pieces; and Handley House, in 6 x 8-inch sheets. Most of these vendors also have channel-shaped trim to support the lattice.

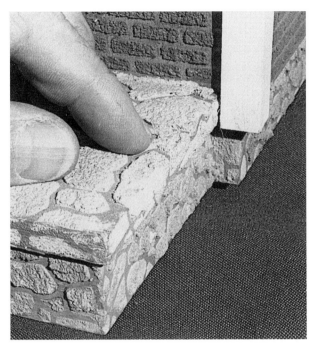

Fig. 10-19. Magic-Ston can be used for both the floor and foundation of the porch.

Use a razor saw to cut the lattice to the height you need and then frame it with the channels. It might be wise to paint the lattice-work one color and the framework a contrasting color before assembling the two. The finished latticework can be cemented right to the front of the foundation beneath the porch. Before installing the latticework, paint the foundation flat black, so it gives the appearance of a hollow area beneath the porch.

Consider creating a deeper (taller) foundation if you are building a larger Victorian dollhouse. To match the height of the house's foundation (or basement), many of the porches on these houses were at least four steps up from ground level.

FRONT STEPS

If your dollhouse doesn't have a porch but does have a set of front steps, you may want to finish the steps with some unusual materials. These are often the focal point of a miniature home.

Timberbrook offers imitation flagstones that can be cut and fitted for front steps and a small

stoop (or porch). Magic-Slat or Lawbre's square slates can be used to simulate another common porch material. Square tiles, in real clay, are available from Houseworks and Miniature House. Paint the tiles with several coats of clear gloss and cement them to the porch (or stoop) and add mortar, as described in Chapter 6. Individual bricks, from Houseworks or Miniature House, can be used to duplicate any brick pattern you might find on a real front porch.

Many of the porches on Victorian-era homes had wooden steps with open, lattice-covered backs. Milled-wood sawtooth-shaped stair stringers and treads (steps), are available from Northeastern and Real Life. They can be cut to the lengths you require. The staircase railings intended for dollhouse interiors can be used for porches with four or more steps.

SECOND-STORY PORCHES

Some homes have second-story back porches, a detail seldom modeled because most dollhouses depict the front of the house. To build that type of porch on your dollhouse, you could add a hinged rear wall. Or you could cut window and door openings in the solid back of any front-opening dollhouse kit.

Bill Lankford's two-story store, shown in the color section, has a back-porch landing on the second story. The porch and stairs are similar to those made with Northeastern's sawtooth-shaped stair strings and risers (steps). Similar detail could be added to any two-story dollhouse.

Full-width second-story porches were common in Victorian houses, serving also as a roof for the back porch. Add-on kits for two-story front porches can be used on the back of the doll-house, or you can build your own from the various available porch pillars.

SCREENED PORCHES

I've never seen a screened porch on a dollhouse, but they must exist. A wraparound one would make a wonderfully realistic addition to a farm-house. And a screened porch would also be appropriate on an updated Victorian house.

To make a realistic screen, use dressmaker's

lace tulle. If you can, find black or gray tulle, or dye white tulle. Use a steam iron to press it perfectly flat.

Build a framework from $\frac{1}{32}$ x $\frac{1}{16}$-inch stripwood, which you've painted to match the windows on the house. Add Laser Tech's laser-cut ornate Victorian wood screen doors, or you can cut and assemble your own from Northeastern's milled-wood window-frame shapes.

SOUTHWESTERN-STYLE PORCHES AND PATIOS

A Southwestern-style patio, made by Susie Lim of Barely Big Enough, is pictured in the color section; it's cut from plywood that's been finished to look like adobe. Houseworks and Miniature House make real clay square tiles that can be used for the porch floors. As described in Chapter 6, paint the tiles with several coats of clear gloss before installing them or applying the mortar.

The cactus plants, cow skull and pots on Lim's patio are ceramic accessories from Dragonfly International and are available at dollhouse stores. The table and chairs are from BH Miniatures.

There are photographs in Chapter 2 of Maureen O'Donnell's Southwestern-style dollhouse shells that include patios. The some of the kits and shells from Fantasy Craft, also shown in Chapter 2, include porches and patios as well.

PORCHES FOR OLD-WEST-STYLE STORES

The western-style store is a favorite subject among dollhouse builders. Single-story dollhouses can be easily customized into stores. With the addition of a two-story-tall false front, they make excellent examples of Old West shops. A porch roof enhances the style.

Bill Lankford's two-story store in the color section has a typical Old West–style roof. It's made from a piece of $\frac{1}{8}$-inch plywood, with real corrugated metal cut from a 12 x 12-inch aluminum sheet available from Dee's Delights. The aluminum was painted with Floquil's Box Car

Fig. 10-20. Norm Nielsen used individual bricks to cover this wood chimney.

Red (a brown shade) and Rust (a reddish brown) to look like rusty steel.

The roof is supported with two pieces of .020-inch diameter K & S wire. The wire is cemented, with thickened cyanoacrylate cement, to brackets on the roof that are the backs of pin-style earrings for pierced ears. The wire and earring backs are also painted several shades of reddish and rusty browns.

BRICK AND STONE CHIMNEYS

A classic brick chimney is included in many dollhouse kits, but you must add this detail to any of the bare plywood shells. If you merely want the short length of a chimney protruding from the rooftop, use one of the wood parts made by either Betty's Wooden Miniatures or Houseworks.

BUILDING A CHIMNEY

The basic shape for the outdoor portion of a chimney can be cut from a piece of $\frac{1}{2}$ x 2-inch wood. Use two thicknesses, above the peak of the roof, to produce a 1 x 2-inch chimney. Cap it with a $1\frac{1}{8}$ x $2\frac{1}{8}$-inch piece of $\frac{1}{8}$-inch-thick

Fig. 10-21. Use copper foil or a lead sheet to make the flashing around the chimney.

hardboard. Drill two ½-inch holes into the wood. Cut two pieces of K & S ½-inch aluminum tube to serve as two chimney stacks.

The chimney can be finished with any of the brick or stone techniques described in Chapter 6. The chimney in the photograph in Chapter 6 is a block of ½ x 3-inch wood. It's covered with Magic-Ston on the lower portion and Magic-Brik on the upper. The photo shows part of the brick mask being removed to reveal the brick mortar color.

The simulated concrete bead around the chimney is formed with ¼-inch-square wood. Magic-Ston creates the texture of rough concrete.

REAL BRICK CHIMNEYS

You can also finish a chimney with the real bricks sold by Houseworks and Miniature House. For a striking appearance, shim the wood stack with ⅛ x ¹⁄₃₂-inch wood strips before applying the bricks.

Norm Nielsen used four layers of wood strips on the chimney in the photograph. (See Fig. 10-20.) Each layer is ¹⁄₃₂ inch thicker than the one below. The widest band of bricks protrudes from the chimney wall a full ⅛ inch. When the shape was finished in wood, Norm cemented individual Miniature House bricks to the chimney with clear silicone bathtub caulking. At least one brick on each row was broken so it would fit. When the chimney was complete, mortar was washed over the bricks, as described in Chapter 6.

The area where the chimney joins the roof is detailed with a strip of self-adhesive lead foil. Copper foil, sold by Dee's Delights, could be substituted. Cut a strip ¼ inch wide, crease it down the middle, and wrap it around the chimney, as shown in the photograph. (See Fig. 10-21.)

Fig. 10-22. The Timberbrook Wood Products garage shell kit, with an operating garage door, can be added to any dollhouse.

Cement the strip in place with clear silicone bathtub caulking.

MINIATURE GARAGES

The garage is one of the most unusual doll-house accessories. Most extensions or wings can be customized into a garage by merely cutting, with an electric saber saw or a hand-held jig saw, a 8¹⁄₁₆- x 7-inch hole in the front wall. Frame the opening with trim to match the doors and windows, and leave it "as is" to suggest that the garage door is open and hanging from the rafters. If you want more realism, Timberbrook Products makes a flat-roofed garage shell with a working door that swings upward. (See Fig. 10-22.)

By now, you won't be surprised to learn that there are 1/12-scale, dollhouse-size toys, lawn mowers, garden tools, packing boxes and just about anything else you could imagine stored in a full-size garage.

If you'd like to put a car in the garage, one of dozens of 1/18-scale automobiles would look great since a true 1/12-scale automobile is so large, it may overpower the house. However, if you prefer the 1/12-scale automobiles, they're available in NASCAR race car shapes, which you could paint to resemble a sedan. Shops that sell radio-controlled race cars and parts can supply the body and chassis. If you don't wish to paint the clear plastic car yourself, ask the shop owner if he or she knows an enthusiast willing to do it for a fee.

FINISHING THE INTERIOR

CHAPTER ELEVEN

WINDOWS, DOORS, TRIM, STAIRS AND FIREPLACES

It starts as a stark, raw, plywood box. In time, with your help and care, it becomes a living environment so realistic that you want to ask, "Who forgot to turn off the lights?" You've seen what can be done with the exterior of that plywood box—now let's look at the interior.

Most of the doors, windows and trim are basswood, though Midwest offers a limited selection of mouldings in walnut, mahogany, maple and cherry. Midwest also carries those woods in 1/32, 1/16 and 3/32 x 3 x 24-inch sheets and 24-inch long wood strips (called scale lumber) from 1/16 x 1/16- to 3/8 x 3/8-inch, with rectangular pieces in that same size range. Midwest and Northeastern have a much larger range of sizes in basswood.

FITTING THE WINDOWS

This is the time to double-check the fit of all the windows. Don't glue them in place until the wallpaper or other interior wall finishing has been completed. (See Fig. 11-1.)

The back edge of the window frame should protrude through the wall just far enough to be flush with the interior wall surface. If the window extends too far inward, you can simply wrap the interior trim around the frame.

If the window does not extend inward enough, add strips of 1/8-inch-square wood to extend the frame. The wood strips also fill in the area around the opening in the plywood walls. Usually, a single row of strips is enough, but with some windows and walls two rows are necessary.

The window pictured here is flush with the interior wall, but it could extend into the room another 1/8 inch and still be covered with the trim. This is one of the standard Houseworks windows designed for a 1/2-inch wall. The wall is 3/8-inch plywood with an exterior covering of 1/8-inch-thick milled-wood clapboard siding, producing a 1/2-inch-thick wall.

The interior frame on this window has been cut at a 45-degree angle to make a nice mitered joint at each corner, and it's the style found in farmhouses and some contemporary homes. This type of trim is included with most of the working windows.

Fig. 11-1. Test-fit the window trim but do not glue it in place.

Fig. 11-2. Custom interior doors should have matching trim on inner and outer door frames.

You can upgrade the trim with milled-wood mouldings from Houseworks or Northeastern Scale Models. A Victorian-era window will have an interior frame that looks very much like the exterior frame. The frames usually have a lower sill that's a bit wider than the vertical trim and an upper sill with an ornate cap.

Northeastern sells all the milled-wood pieces needed to make your own windows. If you want a custom-size window, the wood headers, jambs, sills, sashes and outside casings can be cut in a miter box (see Chapter 14). The parts can then be assembled in the same order as ready-made windows. Hobby shops sell .020-inch-thick Evergreen clear styrene plastic that can be cut with a hobby knife to produce glazing for any size or shape window.

INSTALLING DOORS

The doors that lead through the exterior walls must be fitted exactly as described for the windows. The frame must extend through the walls until it's flush with the face of the interior wall. If it isn't, build up the framework and fill in the opening edges with ⅛-inch-square wood.

Few of the kits include interior doors, but you'll find a wide variety made by dollhouse accessory firms. All of the interior doors have wood frames around all four edges, including a lower sill (called a threshold). Few interior doors in real houses have thresholds because they make it difficult to fit wall-to-wall carpeting and install hardwood floors that extend from one room to another.

The lower sill helps to retain the shape of the door and contains the pin where the door pivots to open and close. Test-fit the doors, but do not cut them until the flooring or carpeting is in place. You will want to remove that lower sill. The door frame should extend all the way to the finished floor and can rest on the hardwood or tile flooring. This means you don't need to fit the flooring around the door frame.

Cut the bottom from the vertical door frame so it is almost even with the bottom of the door. Leave about a paper thickness of clearance between the bottom of the frame and the flooring, so you can slide out the flooring if you need to tape wire lighting or wish to redecorate.

Hold the door in a miter box (see Chapter 14) while you cut the frame with a razor saw. Mark the location of the door's bottom pivot pin on the floor and punch a new hole for that pin with a map pin. Try the door and frame to be sure the door swings properly.

DEALING WITH CARPETED FLOORS

If you use carpeting, you'll want to fit it around the vertical door mouldings. The door must be a bit shorter than the molding so it can swing over the carpet's pile. To find out the difference in the heights of the side moldings and the door, hold the door beside the carpet and note how far the pile extends up the frame. With some of the thicker carpets, the door can be left alone and only the center portion of the lower sill removed.

The lower pivot pin may be too short to extend through the carpet. If so, remove the old pin with pliers and make a new one from a common straight pin. Use diagonal cutters to cut the pin to the new length, and use pliers to press it in place in the door.

FITTING THE TRIM

The interior doors on most real houses have identical trim on both sides of the wall. Many dollhouse doors, however, have simplified trim on just one side. Custom interior doors should have matching trim on both inner and outer door frames. (See Fig. 11-2.) Milled-wood strips are available to closely match those on the exterior.

The trim included with some of the doors matches the simple trim supplied with the windows. For more ornate interior door framework,

Fig. 11-3. Assemble the stairs and fit them, but do not glue them in place until after the wallpaper and flooring have been added.

cut new cornices and vertical sides from the Northeastern or Houseworks milled-wood strips. Custom door hinges, doorknobs and lock face plates, some in gold-plated brass, will further upgrade the doors.

Cut the replacement strips with a razor saw in the miter box, using the ornate outside trim as a pattern, and fit the pieces to the inside frame. Don't glue any of the doors or trim in place until the wallpaper, interior painting and floor finishing have been completed.

Decide now if you want to paint the interior doors and trim or stain them. Both finishes have been used in real houses from any period. The wood used for any of the interior doors and trim has a fine grain that will look very realistic after staining and finishing.

INSTALLING STAIRS

Even though the stairs in most kits are designed to fit precisely, it's wise to assemble the railings and check the fit. Do not glue the stairs in place until you've completed the wallpapering and painting. (See Fig. 11-3.) It's easier to install the interior wall coverings and paint the stairs with this assembly sequence.

Most two-story kits include one-piece milled-

Fig. 11-4. Arlene Hines created this entryway. The wallpaper is from Mini Graphics. Arlene added carpet to the Lawbre curved staircase and a balcony in front of the bedrooms.

wood stairs. Some come with individual precut boards for the stair treads, and a few include railings. These midprice stairs are also available as upgrades for the low-cost kits.

The best stair kits feature individual tread boards and railings with turned wood posts. The ornate railings and posts are available as separate pieces, which can be used to upgrade the least expensive stairs.

STAIR LANDINGS

One of the most interesting interior details is a staircase that makes at least one right-angle turn to pause at a landing. That's a far more common style in full-size homes than the straight stairs found in most dollhouses.

The stairs in any kit can be modified to include a landing. For a simple one, cut the

stairs halfway up. Turn one of the pieces 180 degrees and place it beside the first piece. There will be a small overlapping triangle of wood that can be used to join the two. Glue that joint with carpenter's glue.

Mark the shape of the landing on a piece of ¼-inch plywood. The length should be about 3 inches. The landing's width must be equal to the width of those side-by-side stairs. Using an electric saber saw or a hand-held coping saw, cut the landing from the plywood.

Make supporting walls from ¼-inch plywood. The landing can be supported simply by a box the size of its floor, or the walls can extend beneath the two flights of stairs. Cut a short door in the landing, and consider it an entry to a coat closet.

Custom-made stairs with landings are available from Lawbre and Timberbrook, complete

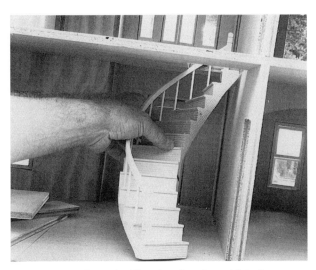

Fig. 11-5. The "standard" ceiling height is 10 inches, so most custom stairs, like these Houseworks curved stairs, are designed to reach that height.

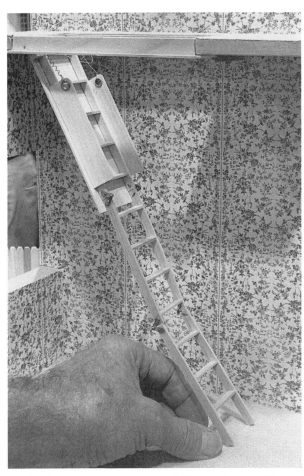

Fig. 11-6. Save floor space in a dollhouse by installing these Timberbrook ready-to-use folding attic stairs.

with turned wood posts. Plastruct makes a four-step style with the steps spread in a fan, so the top step is 90 degrees from the bottom one. A pair of these could be used to create a low-level landing at the foot of a straight staircase.

CURVED AND SPIRAL STAIRS

Kits to build curved stairs are available from Miniature House and Lawbre, which also offer a choice of right- or left-turning curves. (See Fig. 11-4.) The standard ceiling height is 10 inches, so most custom stairs, like the Houseworks curved stairs, are designed to reach that height. However, the upper- or lower-story walls must usually be modified to fit curved stairs because the stairs end 90 degrees from the starting direction. The dollhouse in the photograph, for example, would need a new doorway or archway cut at the top of the stairs to allow for the curved staircase. (See Fig. 11-5.)

Spiral stairs—the compact type that twist around a center post—are a good choice for stairs leading to attic rooms and for townhouse-style interiors. AMSI's ready-to-install metal stairs come in a choice of a simple iron strip style or more ornate simulated wrought iron. The assembled Plastruct variety is a one-piece plastic

moulding that represents precast concrete stairs.

Folding attic stairs for dollhouses are available from Timberbrook. (See Fig. 11-6.) The assembled stairs fold upward, just like real attic stairs. They're an obvious choice to provide visible access to an attic, without using the space of a conventional staircase.

ADDING A FIREPLACE

The fireplace is almost a standard miniature accessory, and it doesn't require any modifications. It's merely an addition, much like a piece of furniture. (See Fig. 11-7 on page 108.) If you can imagine a fireplace style, there is probably a replica available in l/12-scale. You can choose

Fig. 11-7. You can install a fireplace, like this Houseworks miniature, in any dollhouse. A chimney isn't necessary.

Fig. 11-8. Fireplaces are included in most of the Greenleaf kits. The stripes on the walls are Elect-A-Lite tape wires for lighting.

from ornate Victorian wood, simulated cast-metal, brick early-American and an array of ornate Provincial-style fireplaces. The fireplace in a dollhouse, like those in many real homes, could also be an imitation unit with an electric log.

You may want to add some other details that would not appear on most dollhouses. For instance, a real wood-burning fireplace needs a chimney. That's primarily an exterior detail, as described in Chapter 6. In many real houses, however, the brick fireplace extends up the interior wall as well—a detail seldom re-created in a dollhouse.

Simulate the interior portion with a single thickness of bricks running up the inside wall to the ceiling, perhaps a half brick wider than the fireplace. In many real houses, the bricks are covered with plaster. That's easy enough to simulate with a simple piece of ⅛-inch plywood about ⅛ inch wider than your fireplace.

Several of the die-cut Greenleaf dollhouses include fireplaces, and some even have extensions to suggest the presence of the chimney. (See Fig. 11-8.) Few dollhouse builders opt for this style, but it's quite common in real houses. The shelf above the fireplace is a particularly nice touch.

The chimney wall should appear to extend through the ceiling and the second floor. On the second floor, the chimney is almost always encased in plaster, and can be simulated with a simple piece of ⅛-inch plywood. This presents the opportunity of providing a fireplace for a second-floor bedroom, another seldom-duplicated architectural element of a real house.

Cir-Kit and other firms offer simulated flickering fires, powered by the standard 12-volt dollhouse interior-lighting systems. Fireplace screens, andirons and tools are also available from several manufacturers.

CHAPTER TWELVE

LAMPS AND LIGHTING

The real drama in a dollhouse is the lighting. The glow of dozens of little lamps suggests—almost insists—that someone just left the room. You find yourself searching each of the rooms, in turn, to see where that someone might have gone.

LIGHTING FOR EFFECT

You'll certainly want to accent more than one area of a room with lighting. Most of the lighting comes from the open back of the dollhouse, and some may come from an open window. You may want to place the lamps and overhead lighting to complement those primary sources.

You have complete freedom to choose which portions of the room you want to highlight. You might want a kitchen to have an even illumination throughout the room. A table lamp in a library or living room might call attention to an end table with an open book, a glass, a coaster and a pair of eyeglasses.

There's a practical aspect to lighting a dollhouse, too. Even with the large windows and open back, the individual rooms have relatively dark corners. That once-somber shadowy corner becomes the focal point of the room, thanks to the glow from a miniature table or floor lamp.

The most interesting effects are produced when the external lights are turned off or dimmed. In the room where the dollhouse will be displayed, it's worthwhile to replace the wall switch with one that incorporates a dimmer. Dim the room lights and turn the dollhouse lights on—it's a breathtaking sight. Each room draws your attention and becomes a complete environment. You feel like you're looking at a motion picture of a room, that you're close enough to actually step right into it.

That kind of drama can be evoked only with a well-detailed room scene. Proper lighting, however, can transform even a simple setting into a room you'd like to live in.

SAFE LIGHTING SYSTEMS

It's relatively simple to achieve these dramatic lighting effects, thanks to some special wiring systems developed just for dollhouses. Each system runs two wires to each lighting fixture or wall outlet.

Wall outlet? Yes, most of the lamps and fixtures have a two-prong plug. You can purchase miniature sockets, or you can install a pair of eyelets in any part of the wiring and plug into a wall. These plugs, however, are a bit oversize; about the size of a half-gallon milk carton in 1/12-scale. Much smaller plugs and matching wall outlets are available from Cir-Kit Concepts.

All of these systems utilize only 12-volt direct current in the dollhouse; the potentially dangerous 115-volt household current is never touched. A transformer plugs into the wall and converts household current into the lower voltage.

There's a whole range of lighting fixtures offered by many dollhouse accessory manufacturers. Most of the lighting is sold as exact-scale miniature table or floor lamps or ceiling or wall fixtures, each with a replaceable bulb. A few

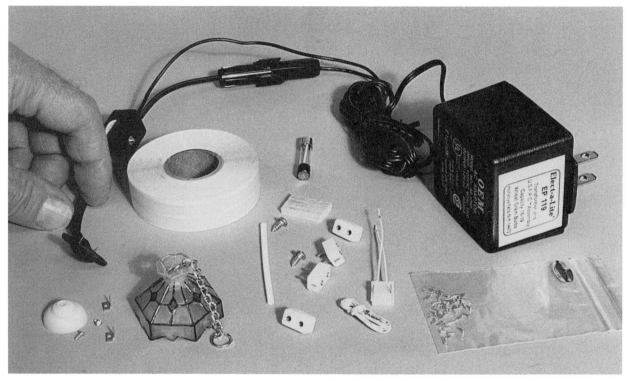

Fig. 12-1. The Elect-A-Lite wiring kit includes enough tape wire to add lighting to the average-size dollhouse.

bare bulbs, with mounting brackets, are available for those who want to design custom lighting systems for contemporary dollhouses. Essentially, a dollhouse is illuminated just the way you would light up a real house—except the miniature bulbs are 12-volt.

TYPES OF LIGHTING SYSTEMS

The traditional method of lighting a dollhouse, using small insulated wires, is just one possibility. Houseworks and Cir-Kit offer what the industry calls round-wire systems. A groove must be cut in the dollhouse walls or ceilings so the wires can be "buried" beneath wallpaper or a layer of tape and paint.

There are also two types of flat-tape wiring that use two rows of copper foil as the wire and are embedded in self-stick plastic tape. Elect-A-Lite's system has two copper strips on top of a single piece of tape; with Cir-Kit's system, the

copper strips are sandwiched between two layers of tape. The copper tape is at least as efficient a conductor of electricity as the small round wires. The industry usually refers to these as "tape wire systems."

The advantage of both brands of tape wire systems is that the tape can be placed right on the walls or ceilings and covered with paint or wallpaper. Also, there's very little fiddling with bare wires. Most of the wire junctions and some lighting fixtures are installed with push-in ⅛-inch brass nails called brads.

Usually, the lighting fixtures merely plug into the tape. Each fixture has a pair of sharp points that penetrate the tape, thus making an electrical connection. Some fixtures have two stranded wires that must be attached to a dime-size adapter, which, in turn, is pressed into the tape.

Wall outlet sockets can be installed easily— just push them into the wall with one prong through each of the copper strips. There's even a working on-off switch that can be plugged into the tape. What's more, you can install any of these lighting fixtures, sockets or lamps after the interior is completely finished with paint and/or wallpaper.

TAPE WIRING SYSTEMS

Dollhouse builders who prefer the Cir-Kit system claim there is an advantage in having the both sides of the copper foil covered by plastic tape. They feel that the tape protects the thin copper strips so they are less vulnerable to accidental scratching or cuts.

Those who prefer Elect-A-Lite's system claim that their thinner, single-layer tape is less obtrusive beneath paint or wallpaper. They also feel that there is a better chance of the brass brads carrying the current, because there's less plastic to act as possible insulation between the brad and the copper. Elect-A-Lite also offers an optional two-layer tape.

Both systems are similar enough so that you can use the same general installation procedure. Both have starter kits that include a transformer (to reduce 115-volt household current to a safe 12 volts), a wire and plug-in connector to connect the dollhouse to the transformer, a roll of the two-copper strip tape, a test probe, a sample lightbulb, brads and full instructions. (See Fig. 12-1.) Elect-A-Lite has a paper practice board for hands-on learning as well as a lamp and two of the oversize plugs and sockets. Cir-Kit includes a pencil-size Pilot Hole Punch to create the holes for the brads so they're easy to install. Those items are, of course, available as separate pieces.

The Cir-Kit 34-page Tape Wire Instruction Book, included with the kit, is also sold separately. I suggest you pick up a copy, regardless of which brand of tape you buy. This chapter provides most of the information you need to wire a dollhouse, but the booklet offers some additional tricks and explains special wiring circuits.

Basic Wiring Circuit

The basic wiring circuit for a tape wire house routes the electric current from the transformer through the wires to a medium-size two-pin plug and socket. Cir-Kit calls their plug and socket a junction splice; Elect-A-Lite calls theirs a transformer end plug. The junction splice has two

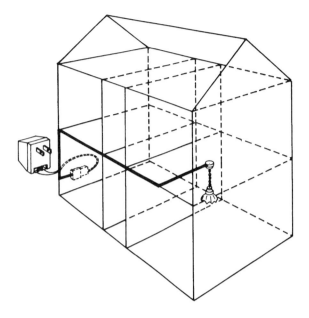

Fig. 12-2. Follow this general pattern to route tape wires to each light. **Courtesy Cir-Kit Concepts.**

sharp pins that are to be driven through the tape wire to bring the current into the house.

The tape wire is run up and across the walls, across the edges of the floors and over the ceilings to the lights. In the diagram, only a single overhead fixture is in place, so you can see the direct path of the electric current through the tape wire. (See Fig. 12-2.)

The tape wire is the source of electric current for every light. That means you can locate a light only where you have tape wire. Fortunately, you can plug in a light anywhere on the tape. It takes some planning to decide where to run the wires. You may already know precisely where you want each ceiling light fixture (if any) and about where you want to locate each lamp. Still, it's wise to give yourself some options.

In most rooms, it's best to run a strip of tape wire the full width of at least one wall. You then have a choice of many locations for table and floor lamps. If you think you might want a ceiling light fixture, run the tape up there and leave it. You may discover that you need four or five lights in some rooms to get the desired level of brightness.

Create a standard wiring location for the tape

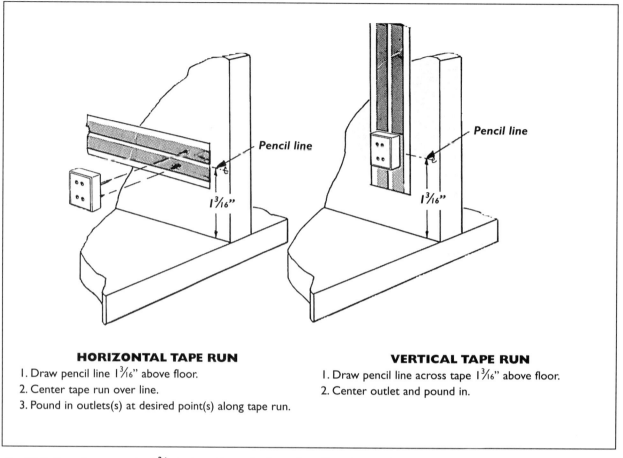

HORIZONTAL TAPE RUN

1. Draw pencil line 1³⁄₁₆" above floor.
2. Center tape run over line.
3. Pound in outlets(s) at desired point(s) along tape run.

VERTICAL TAPE RUN

1. Draw pencil line across tape 1³⁄₁₆" above floor.
2. Center outlet and pound in.

*Fig. 12-3. Run the tape wire 1³⁄₁₆-inch up from the floor. Install outlets at that same height. **Courtesy Cir-Kit Concepts.***

wire, and use it in every room. The horizontal tape wire should be located precisely 1³⁄₁₆ inches above the floor, so you know exactly where it is even when it's covered by wallpaper. That also places any outlets at a 1/12-scale distance above the floor. The small box shown in the drawing is the outlet to accept Cir-Kit 1004 or 1004-2 scale-size two-prong electrical plugs. (See Fig. 12-3.)

Similarly, run any wires that are near doorways 1³⁄₁₆ inches away from the finished doorjamb. If you want to install a wall switch or a sconce later, you'll know precisely where the tape is located.

It's wise to wait at least a week before concluding that you've installed all the tape wires you'll ever need. If possible, buy or borrow the light fixtures you want and place them in the room to give some idea of where the light will be.

Consider lighting with sconces, which provide the light of a table lamp without the complication of positioning the cord so it's unobtrusive. Decide if you want lighting in the attic rooms, and if you want to install working porch lights or carriage lamps on the exterior walls.

Preparing to Wire

Decide now if there's a chance you'll want to simulate painted plaster in any room. If so, the walls must be painted with wood sealer or sanding sealer and sanded smooth. Two or three coats may be necessary to hide all traces of the wood grain. If you are going to paper the walls, a single

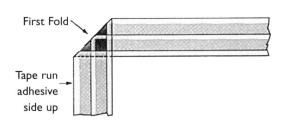
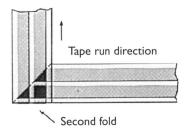

Fig. 12-4. Folding the tape wire to make a no-splice right turn requires two steps. **Courtesy Cir-Kit Concepts.**

coat is enough to seal the walls and provide a smooth enough surface for the tape wire.

Use a pencil and ruler to mark the locations of the centerlines of all the tape wires. It's easier to erase and redraw pencil lines than to remove and replace the tape wires. You now have the chance to put all the tape wire just where you want it, so five years from now, you can add a wall sconce beside the fireplace without installing more tape wire. Of course, after the interior is finished you can always run a strip of tape and simply repaint or repaper that wall.

Some dollhouse builders advise placing the tape wire on the ceiling to reach ceiling fixtures, but I suggest you put it on the floor of the room above. Install any flooring on the second or third story with double-stick carpet tape, as shown in Chapter 14. That way, wood floors, tiles and carpets can be pried up for access to the tape wire (or round wiring) if you need to correct a location or add wiring.

Installing the Tape Wire

Tape wire has a paper backing that must be removed before applying it. Remove the backing only when you are actually sticking down the tape. Tear off any excess backing, but don't cut the tape wire until you have run it as far through the house as possible. Fewer splices create less chance for errors.

The walls should be painted with at least one coat of sealer, paint or even wallpaper paste so the tape wire will stick. Use your finger to push the tape wire firmly into place. Use a credit card—never your fingernail—to push the tape into corners. Particularly with Elect-A-Lite tape wire, a curved corner leaves the bare copper exposed for a short distance.

The tape wire will not curve sideways. When you want to make a right-angle turn, make two diagonal folds as shown in the drawings. (See Fig. 12-4.) First, fold the tape wire back over itself, sticky side up at a 45-degree angle. Next, fold the tape wire back over itself again at a 45-degree angle. The second fold will put the sticky side back down and the tape wire will run off at a 90-degree right angle to the original direction.

Practice the technique with a short piece of the tape wire so you'll be able to make either right or left turns. If you make the first and second folds 22 degrees, the tape wire can be turned at a shallow 135-degree angle.

Forming a T-junction

At any point where a piece of tape wire branches off the main route, forming a T-junction, you will need to join two pieces of tape. This is the place where short circuits often occur, so be careful. Also see the discussion "Avoiding Short Circuits" later in this chapter.

The Cir-Kit tape wire has two colors: One strip is the standard orange color of copper, and the other is a metallic blue. This helps prevents short circuits because you are not as likely to drive a brad through an orange and blue pile as you are through the proper pile of two oranges or two blues.

To make a splice that joins tapes branching

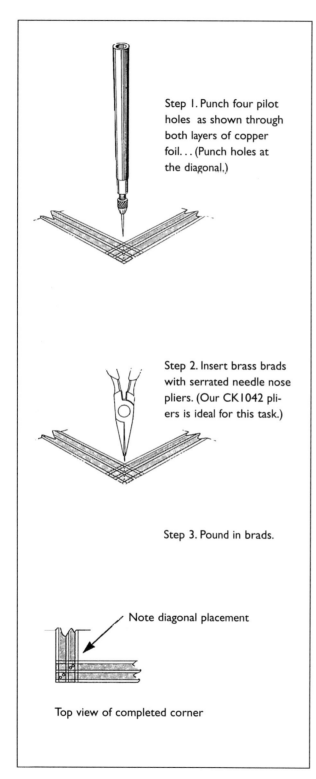

Step 1. Punch four pilot holes as shown through both layers of copper foil... (Punch holes at the diagonal.)

Step 2. Insert brass brads with serrated needle nose pliers. (Our CK1042 pliers is ideal for this task.)

Step 3. Pound in brads.

Note diagonal placement

Top view of completed corner

Fig. 12-5. Use three steps to make a splice that joins tapes branching from T-Junctions. Courtesy Cir-Kit Concepts.

from T-Junctions, put the tape wire in place and press it down firmly. Use the Cir-Kit Pilot Hole Punch to make two diagonal holes in each run of tape wire. (See Fig. 12-5.) Press four brass brads firmly into the holes, and the splice or T-junction is complete.

Two extra, precautionary steps are needed to join Elect-A-Lite tape wires at a T-junction, or splice, because the copper tape is exposed on one side. Push one of the squares of Elect-A-Lite white tape over the copper strips that will be on the inside of the T. (See Fig. 12-6.) This will keep that strip from any accidental electrical contact with the second strip. Complete the T-junction and drive in the four brads. Cover the junction with a second square of white tape. Tape wire can be routed from junction splices to wall outlets and ceiling fixtures. (See Fig. 12-7.)

Tape Wire for Ceiling Fixtures

The tape wire must reach the center of the ceiling when a ceiling light fixture is to be installed there. The tape wire can be run right across the ceiling, but some dollhouse builders feel that it's best to run it across the floor above. Then, the tape wire can be accessed by prying up the flooring, tiles or carpeting (assuming it's installed with double-sided carpet tape).

There are a couple of potential problems with locating the tape on the ceiling: The fixture may have its own mounting bracket that must be mounted right over the top of the tape wire. If you are attaching these fixtures with the brads through the tape, you can easily tear the tape. And the weight of the fixtures may pull the tape away from the ceiling.

The photograph illustrates one way to run tape wires on the floor. To locate the position of the fixture, measure the ceiling to find the center of the room. Mark that location and drill a $1/16$-inch hole, which will provide a position for the tape on the floor above. Push the tape down, then drill the hole on through the tape wire. The wires from the fixture will also be pushed through the hole when the fixture is installed.

Avoiding Short Circuits

There's always the possibility of a short circuit when working with any wiring system. Cir-Kit and Elect-A-Lite include replaceable or reset-

Fig. 12-6. Insert two squares of white insulating tape between the folds of Elect-A-Lite tape wires.

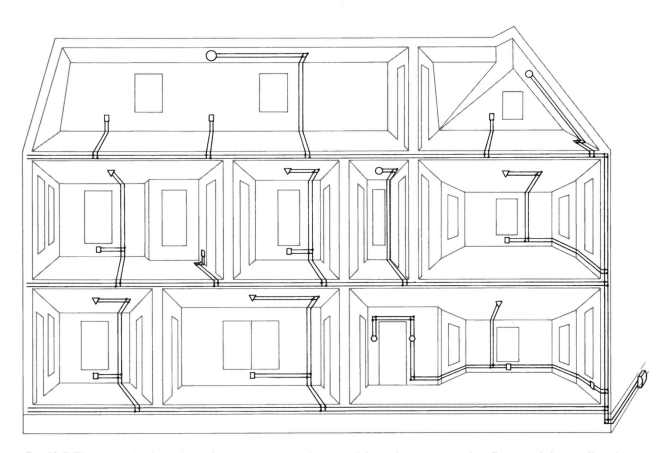

Fig. 12-7. This example shows how the tape wires can be routed from the junction splice (lower right) to wall outlets and ceiling fixtures. Note that wall outlets can be placed anywhere around the two walls of the lower right room. **Courtesy Cir-Kit Concepts.**

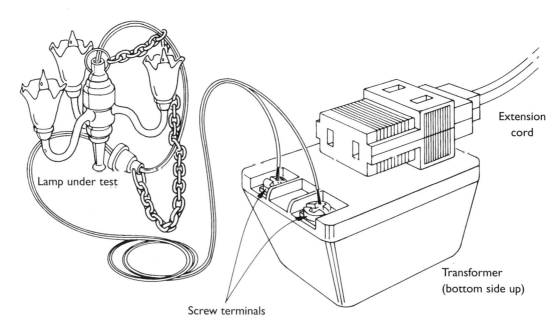

Lamp under test

Extension cord

Transformer (bottom side up)

Screw terminals

Fig. 12-8. Touch the bare wire ends from each lamp or fixture to the terminals of the transformer to check for short circuits. Courtesy Cir-Kit Concepts.

table circuit breakers, but a short circuit can still destroy part of the tape wiring. It follows that the first rule of wiring is to avoid short circuits.

The most likely sources of short circuits are the lamps and lighting fixtures, not the wiring. Before you install any fixture, test it by touching the wires to the terminals of the transformer. (See Fig. 12-8.) If the bulb burns or flickers to a very bright intensity, check for a break in the wire or replace the fixture.

Also, check the wiring as you connect each new piece of tape wire. Use the circuit tester to be certain there's no chance for a short circuit up to that point. (See Fig. 12-9.) Be sure the transformer is plugged in and the circuit breaker is not out. The junction splice (which connects the transformer to the tape wire) must be firmly in place. Push the pins of the test probes into the tape wires, and the test lamp should glow. Try the test probe at every tape wire run, especially where you will be installing lights or wall outlets.

The points where the tape wires form a T-junction are also sources of short circuits. It's all too easy to drive the brads into the copper strips with different polarities. Cir-Kit's two-color tape

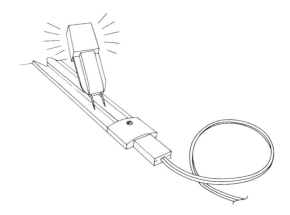

Fig. 12-9. The circuit-tester pins will reach right through paint or wallpaper to the tape wire. Courtesy Cir-Kit Concepts.

wire helps here. It also helps to remember the rule that the brads must be located on diagonally crossing pieces of tape wire: Think "upper right/lower left."

Installing Light Fixtures

Some light fixtures are prewired to their installation pins. Push the two sharp pins into the tape wire (with the light positioned so one pin pushes

Fig. 12-10. Use these three steps to connect a table lamp to the tape wire: Punch two holes with a map pin or pushpin, push the bare lamp wires into the holes, and secure the wires with two brass brads pressed into the holes. This is less obtrusive than inserting eyelets into the tape wire to serve as sockets for the oversize plugs. **Courtesy Cir-Kit Concepts.**

Fig. 12-11. The Cir-Kit adapter plate for ceiling fixtures is a dime-size plastic disc (center). The brass lamp-hanging fixture twists into the adapter, and the fixture hangs from the brass hanger.

into each of the two copper strips), and the light should glow. Cir-Kit makes a small adapter plate for plugging in wall sconces, and many of the Clare Bell sconces are designed to plug into them. Cir-Kit has their own series of adaptable sconces and ceiling fixtures.

To install lights that have only two wires, use your fingernail to carefully strip the insulation from each of the lamp wires. Hold the wire between your forefinger and press your thumbnail firmly into the insulation. Pull the wire, and the insulation should break. Then pull the insulation from the wire, rotating it so the individual strands of wire will twist into a neat rope.

Punch a hole in each of the copper strips in the tape wires with a common pushpin. (See Fig. 12-10.) Push one of the bare wire ends into one hole, and the second bare wire end into the second hole. Carefully tap a brad into each hole to trap the wire firmly against the copper tape.

Install the ceiling fixtures or wall sockets after you've completed painting and wallpapering. If you are uncertain that you'll be able to locate the connections after the tape wire is covered, push brads into holes made with the pushpin. The heads of the brads will be visible

through any amount of paint or wet wallpaper. You can remove the brads and install the wires and lights after the wallpaper, flooring and ceiling treatment have been completed.

To install the actual chandelier or ceiling fixture, the tape wire to reach the ceiling fixture must, of course, be in place, either on the ceiling itself or on the floor directly above the fixture. If it's on the floor, you will have drilled a $\frac{1}{16}$-inch hole to accept the wires from the fixture. You won't need to drill the hole if the tape wire is on the ceiling.

Use the pushpin to make a hole in each of the copper tapes, then strip the insulation. Push the two wires through the $\frac{1}{16}$-inch hole in the ceiling and into the holes you just punched in the tape wire, followed with the brass brads. The fixture can then be installed with brads or small screws.

Cir-Kit's ceiling fixtures have an inner and outer set of adapter plates. (See Fig. 12-11.) The inner one is installed simply by pushing it into the copper tape wire. The wires from the lamp must be stripped of insulation and attached to the outer adapter plate with the eyelets or tiny screws provided. The outer adapter, including the light fixture, is then pushed over the inner adapter and twisted to lock it in place.

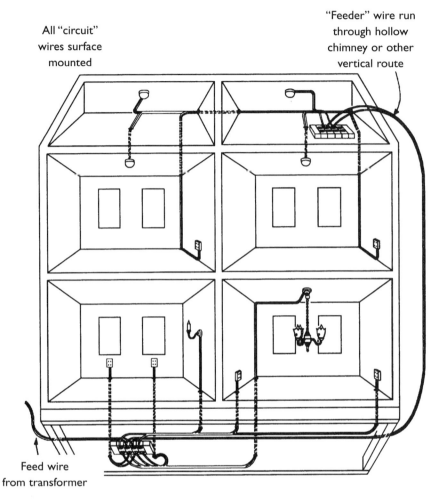

All "circuit"
wires surface
mounted

"Feeder" wire run
through hollow
chimney or other
vertical route

Feed wire
from transformer

Fig. 12-12. Route conventional round wires in corners and hide them behind baseboards. These wires lead to two terminal blocks, one in the attic and the second in the foundation. The terminal blocks minimize the number of wire splices needed. Courtesy Cir-Kit Concepts.

CONVENTIONAL WIRING SYSTEMS

The conventional, or round wire, dollhouse wiring systems use the same transformers as the tape wire systems to reduce 115-volt household electrical current to a harmless 12 volts. The wires from the transformer, however, may lead directly into the dollhouse.

Most dollhouse builders who use the round wire system, available from Cir-Kit and Houseworks, also install an on-off switch between the transformer and the dollhouse. Some include a terminal block so the wires from the dollhouse can be attached with screws,

allowing additional wires to be installed at some later time.

The Houseworks system includes large plugs and sockets that match those supplied on most sconces and table and floor lamps. Additional plugs and sockets are installed by inserting the wires into eyelets and then into the plugs or sockets. This makes long extension cords that connect all the lighting to a single 12-volt power source. Such a system is handy for very small dollhouses with only six to twelve light fixtures. More complex wiring could be accomplished with two or three of these systems.

If you are used to working with wiring on a

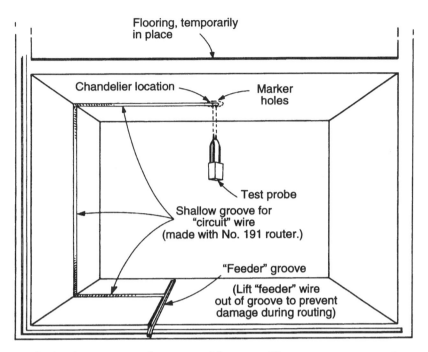

Flooring, temporarily
in place

Chandelier location

Marker
holes

Test probe

Shallow groove for
"circuit" wire
(made with No. 191 router.)

"Feeder" groove

(Lift "feeder" wire
out of groove to prevent
damage during routing)

Fig. 12-13. Hide round wires in grooves in these general locations. The grooves are cut with a router bit in a motor tool. **Courtesy Cir-Kit Concepts.**

model railroad or in assembling electronics hobby kits, you may prefer the conventional wiring in the Cir-Kit Round Wire kits. Each of the wire T-joints is made by stripping the insulation from the wires, twisting the wires together, and then covering the joints with insulated tape or heat-shrink tubing.

Cir-Kit's 104 Round Wire Kit includes a transformer with circuit breaker, a lead-in wire with on-off switch, 15 feet of wire, two four-wire terminal blocks, pins and grommets to make wire connections, and a 67-page *Round Wire Instruction Book*. The book is also sold separately, and I urge you to buy it if you're considering the use of a round wire system.

The Cir-Kit system uses inexpensive headless pins to connect the bare wires of the individual lights to the feeder wires that lead to the transformer. The pins allow the connections to be made without using solder, insulated tape or heat shrink tubing. With the use of a few terminal blocks, no wire joints are necessary.

The system does require cutting many notch-es and grooves in the walls to hide the wires and joints with the lights or outlets. The finished appearance, however, is as satisfactory as that of the tape wire systems.

If you would rather not cut grooves, the round wires can sometimes be routed behind curtains, down corners or beneath rugs to hide them from casual view. The wires can all be routed downward through the dollhouse and directly into the foundation area. There, they can be attached to the terminal blocks and connected in turn to the 12-volt transformer. Again, the system is most practical when there are no more than about a dozen lights or outlets.

Study the round wire lighting drawing. (See Fig. 12-12.) The wire routing and terminal block areas would be similar to the plug-and-socket wiring system sold by Houseworks. For a realistic room, the wires should be buried in slots in the walls, floor or ceiling. The grooves are cut with a 191 router bit used in one of the Dremel or Foredom motor tools sold at larger hobby stores. (See Fig. 12-13.)

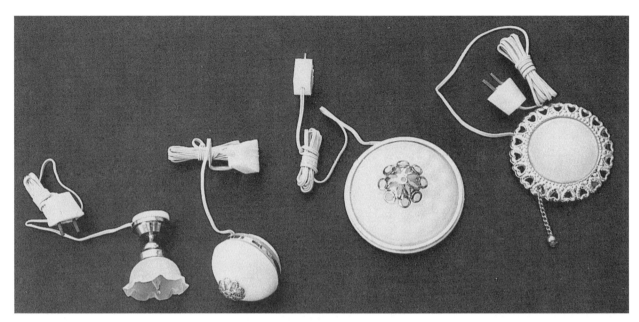

Fig. 12-14. The fixtures pictured here are (left to right) Miniature House's 650 Tulip Shade, 681 Small Globe, 684 Large Globe and 729 Gold Heart Trim (with a nonworking pull chain). Each includes one of the inner and outer adapters so the fixture can be removed easily to change bulbs.

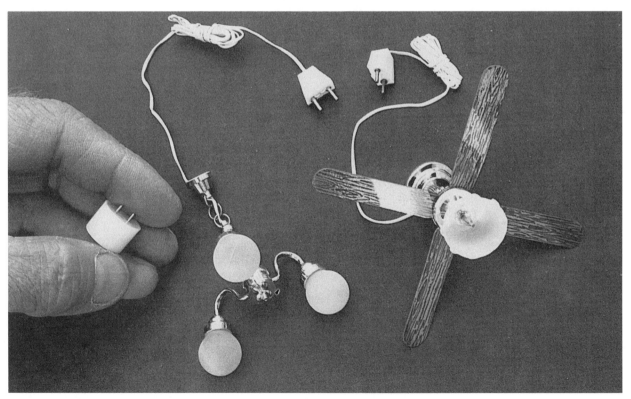

Fig. 12-15. The simplest ceiling fixture (far left) is the Cir-Kit Ceiling Globe. To install it, just push it into the tape wire. More ornate chandeliers and ceiling fans are also available; Miniature House's 719 Deluxe Lighted Ceiling Fan is shown here.

WHAT'S AVAILABLE IN MINIATURE

There is an incredible array of ceiling light fixtures available. (See Fig. 12-14.) If it exists in real life, chances are some dollhouse manufacturer has a near replica. You can even buy Christmas lights to trim a miniature tree or house. You'll find 1½-inch-long frosted glass "Fluorette" bulbs and mounting clips that look and shine like fluorescent lights as well as scale-size candles with plug-in replacement bulbs. The candles can be used in most Victorian-era fixtures in place of standard bulbs.

A more modern dollhouse might be illuminated with simpler fixtures, such as the Cir-Kit 841 Large Pin-In Ceiling Globe. This self-contained light fixture has a tiny bulb inside. To install it, just push it firmly into the tape wire. (See Fig. 12-15.) For such a small ceiling fixture, it would be wise to run the tape wire on the ceiling, rather than the floor above. Similar "bare bulb" simulated porcelain fixtures are available from Cir-Kit.

Larger ceiling fixtures should be installed, as mentioned before, with the tape on the floor above. Cir-Kit's 857 3-Arm Globe Chandelier is an example of a relatively simple chandelier. More ornate fixtures, which use plastic to simulate cut glass, are made by other manufacturers. Several ceiling fans are also available.

Dollhouse manufacturers usually include a wire and plug with wall sconces. Just as it might be done in a real house, you can run the wire down the wall to a socket on the tape wire strip near the baseboard. These fixtures can also be installed on the Cir-Kit inner and outer adapters so they simply plug into the tape wire. There are plenty of options in sconces, including tulip styles and carriage lamps. (See Fig. 12-16 and Fig. 12-17.)

Many real houses were never wired for ceiling lamps, but there are enough miniature table and floor lamps available so you can duplicate that style of lighting in just about any era or decor. (See Fig. 12-19 and Fig. 12-20.) If possible, position the lamps approximately where they will be when the room is furnished. You may then be able to decide if you need to add a strip of tape wire to another wall in order to provide for additional outlets.

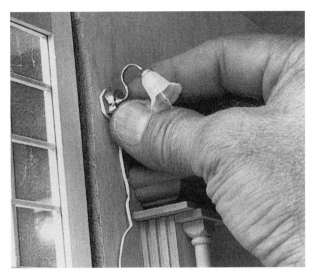

Fig. 12-16. Mount tulip-style wall sconces with the bulb pointing down or up. The sconce can be pushed into the wall and its electrical cord plugged into a baseboard tape wire.

WORKING WALL SWITCHES

A working wall switch, from Elect-A-Lite and Cir-Kit, is a nice touch. The switch itself is a scale-size two-lever wall switch. (See Fig. 12-18 on page 122.) The little levers are molded, and the back has two pins to plug into the tape wire. To turn lights on or off, the entire switch box is moved up or down the wall about ¹⁄₆₄ inch. Internal sliding contacts turn the electrical power on and off.

To include a working on-off switch in the circuit to a ceiling fixture, the wall switch must be placed on the tape wire leading to one ceiling fixture only. Cut a ¹⁄₁₆-inch chunk from the tape wire, and place the wall switch on the tape wire to bridge the gap. Full instructions are furnished with the wall switches, including alternative tape wire connections.

PLUG-IN LAMP CORDS

Table lamps have large, prewired plugs that can be used with brass ⅛-inch eyelets, such as Cir-Kit's number 1023. Make a starter hole for the eyelets with a small awl or ice pick. Push one eyelet into one of the copper tapes and the other into the second tape, spaced to match the prongs on the plugs.

The Cir-Kit 1005 or 1004-2 plugs are much

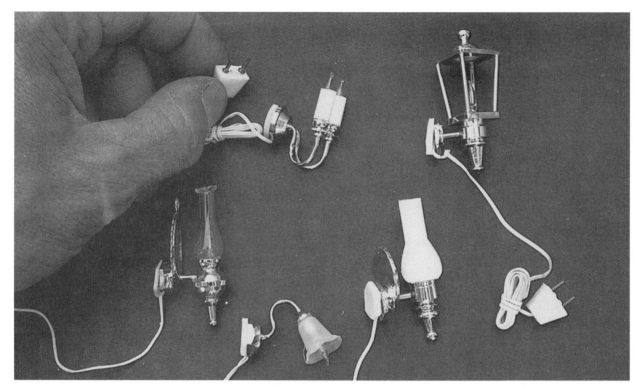

Fig. 12-17. Dozens of different wall sconces are available, including these from Miniature House: 761 Wall Sconce, 640 Canted Tulip Wall Sconce, 606 Wall Lamp with Two Candles and 701 Wall Sconce with Backplate. There is also a selection of outdoor porch lamps, including the 614 Brass Carriage Lamp (right).

smaller than standard ones. They're almost exact l/12-scale replicas of the plugs on full-size table and floor lamps and are designed to plug into the scale-size Cir-Kit 1004 outlet. The outlet, which has two sockets to accept two plugs, is installed by simply pushing it into place on any section of the tape wire.

See the two diagrams with the steps needed to replace oversize plugs with scale-size ones. (See Fig. 12-21 and Fig. 12-22.) The "bulb wires" in the drawings lead from the light fixture to the oversize plug. Cut the wires to remove the plug, then strip the insulation and twist the strands of each wire together. Insert the two stripped lamp wires into the two tiny holes in the back of the 1004 plug. Then insert the two brass pins into the plug and press them firmly in place with pliers. Trim the excess wire protruding from the back of the plug and twist the two insulated wires together.

The plugs can also be removed and the wires cut so the lamps will be permanently con-

nected to a tape wire strip. The technique for this installation is the same as for ceiling fixtures described earlier.

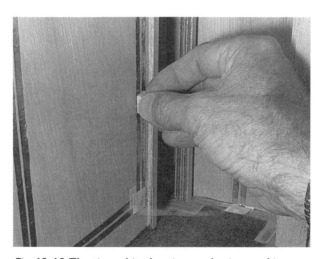

Fig. 12-18. The tiny white box is a scale-size working wall switch. Slide it up or down to turn the lights on or off.

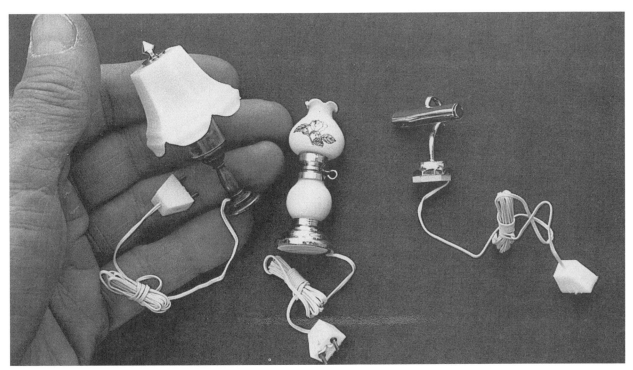

Fig. 12-19. These table lamps are Miniature House's 642 White, 699 Elegant and 708 Brass Desk. The oversize plugs are included on most lamps and fixtures.

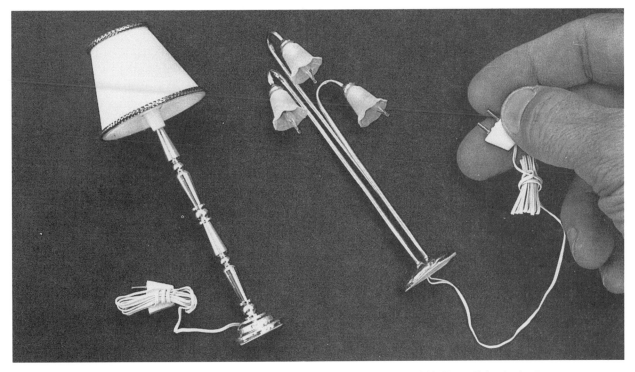

Fig. 12-20. These floor lamps are Miniature House's 718 Gold Tone Base and 712 Three-Tulip Arched.

1. Strip bulb wires back approximately ½".
2. Twist stripped ends to eliminate loose wires.
3. Install bared wire ends into side holes on plug and out holes on back. (Pull insulation flush with side of plug but not into holes.)

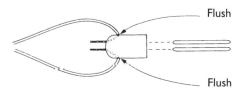

Fig. 12-21. These are the initial steps for inserting the wires into the scale-size Cir-Kit 1004 wall plugs on any dollhouse lamp cord. Courtesy Cir-Kit Concepts.

4. Insert brass pins into front of plug with household-type pliers as shown. Pins should be pushed flush with back of plug.

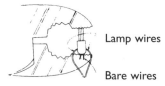

5. Clip bare wires protruding through back of plug with fingernail clipper.

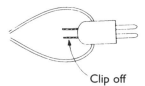

6. Twist lamp wire for finished look.

Fig. 12-22. These are the final steps needed to secure the dollhouse lamp cord to the Cir-Kit 1004 scale-size wall plug. Courtesy Cir-Kit Concepts.

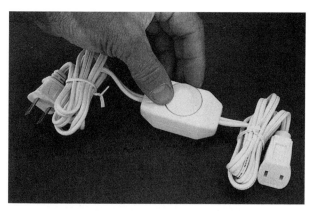

Fig. 12-23. Dollhouse lighting can be lowered to a more realistic glow using an extension cord with a built-in dimmer switch, such as Cir-Kit's 8002, between the wall outlet and the transformer.

DIMMING THE LIGHTS

As small as they might be, the lightbulbs used in dollhouse lamps and fixtures are extremely bright. The effect is similar to that of placing 250-watt bulbs in every lamp in your home, so the lighting will be far more realistic if it's turned down. Hardware stores sell extension cords with built-in dimmer switches, or you can buy the Cir-Kit 8002 from your dollhouse dealer. (See Fig. 12-23.) The rotating switch can be turned to reduce the lights to a mere glow or to increase them to full intensity. The adjustable switch in the cord controls the power going into the transformer. If you turn the lights down low in a Victorian dollhouse, they appear to cast the warm glow of candles.

CHAPTER THIRTEEN

WALLPAPER AND PAINT

For some of us, much of what's been covered in the previous chapters is simply a prelude to the interior. Here's where you can really get your imagination going to create those living spaces. Best of all, affordability isn't a problem when you're decorating in miniature. Neither is availability—you can find dollhouse versions of virtually any interior decor you'd want for a real house.

INTERIOR DECORATING GOALS

Consider your goals in creating a dollhouse. Is it the construction you enjoy most? Decorating the interior? Or just admiring the results of your work? If it's decorating you like, take all the time you can to finish the interior. You may wish to enroll in a decorating course before you select the colors and materials for your dollhouse.

Interior design usually begins with the furniture, so you'll need to know what you want before you can select the materials for the wall coverings and floors. Think about what you'll be using for window treatments and rugs, too. (See Fig. 13-1.)

I suggest that you paint the interior a neutral color to suit your style. Remember that the walls need to be sealed before the wallpaper or final color is applied. If all the walls at least look fin-

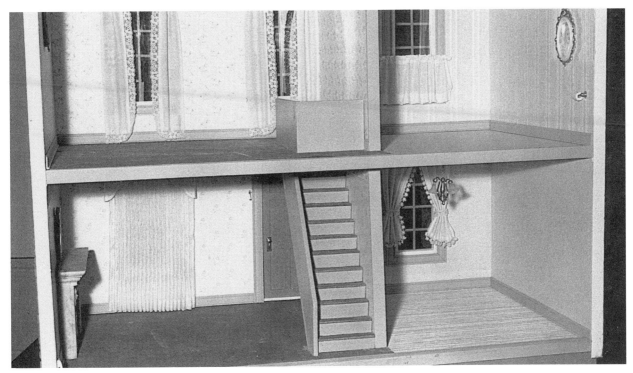

Fig. 13-1. This dollhouse interior has been decorated with carpets, drapes, wallpaper and pictures on the wall.

ished, you won't be in such a rush to decorate just to make the dollhouse look complete.

Some prefer a stark white as a neutral color for walls and ceilings. Others use an eggshell white, and still others go for white with a tint of color. Pick colors for the living room, dining room and bedrooms and, perhaps, another for the bathroom and a third for the kitchen.

If you're not sure whether you want painted or stained doors and interior trim, leave those items alone for now. If you're sure you want to stain them, go ahead and do it. Protect the stain with a clear coat of semi-gloss paint. Then at least those components will look finished. All wood needs to be primed and sanded before painting anyway, so staining won't waste much time even if you decide to paint some or all of the interior trim.

Hold the doors, windows and trim in place temporarily with small dabs of Handcraft Designs' Mini-Hold or Miniature Lumber Shoppe's Hold. These waxlike compounds stick like glue, yet the parts can be easily removed. A pinhead-size dab is usually enough to hold a piece of trim in place.

By the way, this sticky stuff is also great for hanging pictures and for holding details such as lamps, candelabra, clocks or telephones to tables or shelves so they don't get knocked off every time the dollhouse is touched.

PLASTERING THE WALLS

There's no reason to apply plaster to the walls of a dollhouse. The plywood is far smoother than you could ever trowel plaster. To hide the wood grain, paint the walls and ceiling with wood sealer or sanding sealer. Let it dry, then sand the walls with fine-grit sandpaper. Wipe the dust away with a damp rag and apply another coat of sealer. There will probably still be visible grain, so a third coat may be needed. This whole procedure should, of course, take place before you install the wiring.

PAINTING THE WALLS

Interior latex wall paint is fine for any dollhouse interior. If you want a smaller amount, buy 8-ounce jars of dollhouse paints such as New England Hobby Supply's Builder's Choice, Dee's Delights' Art Deco Americana or Borden's Accent. Buy a quality ¾-inch-wide paintbrush, too.

The most important "tool" is adequate working light. Use at least two 200-watt bulbs, in clamp-on reflector fixtures, or lamps without shades. Place the lamps so their light comes from two directions; be sure there are no shadows on either the ceiling or wall you're working on.

The walls should be painted with primer and all the wiring must be in place before you apply the final colors. Remove the windows and trim. The floor is still unfinished, so you don't need to worry about paint drips.

Dip about a third of the paintbrush into the paint and wipe it lightly on the edge of the can or jar. Spread the paint in long, even coats. When you touch the brush to the surface, bring it down in a gentle, curving motion to "feather" the start of the fresh paint. Cover just one wall at a time so you can touch up missed spots or smooth over any runs before the paint dries.

If you are using several colors in the rooms, it might be best to pick a neutral color for the edges of the dollhouse. If the rooms will be relatively dark, paint the edges a medium brown to suggest stained wood. If the interiors will be light, paint the edges a color no brighter than the lightest room.

PAPERING THE WALLS

The range of wallpapers for dollhouses is almost as great as for real houses. You'll find borders, which can be used on either a painted wall or with wallpaper, as well as two-piece patterns with chair rail borders. These can be assembled from a variety of complementary designs. Wallpapers that duplicate hand-painted border stencils are also available. If you want to paint your own stencils, there are more than a dozen different brass stencil patterns available.

The J. Hermes Company even prints a wallpaper that creates the look of old newspapers; it's particularly effective in attic areas. Apply the paper to the ceilings of the attic as described on page 127 for walls. Simulate the exposed roof rafters with strips of ⅛ x ½-inch basswood. Spray

Fig. 13-2. Jennifer Samsow decorated this attic room with J. Hermes Old Newspaper wallpaper.

the wood with clear flat paint so it doesn't yellow. Cement the strips over the wallpaper with a thin bead of clear silicone bathtub caulking compound. Jennifer Samsow built a small diorama depicting a similar attic scene. (See Fig. 13-2.)

Once you've mastered the techniques for installing wallpaper, you may want to use wallpaper fairly often. It's available in solid colors, so you can use it in place of paint. Some dollhouse builders feel that it's easier to apply wallpaper to simulate plaster than to attempt to paint over the plywood and sand away all traces of wood grain. Wallpaper hides the tape wire more easily than paint alone does.

WALLPAPERING BASICS

Clear a flat work surface, at least 24 x 48 inches, to lay the wallpaper on when applying the paste. You will also need a large bowl or bucket of water and three or four sponges for cleanup.

Wallpapers are usually prepasted, but it's best to apply paste anyway. Dollhouse stores sell several brands, including Handcraft Designs' E-Z Hold and Mini Graphics' Wallpaper Mucilage. Buy a small plastic syringe and fill it with the paste. Use a 2-inch-wide paint sponge to apply the paste so no paintbrush hairs will appear behind the wallpaper.

You'll also need a 3-foot-long steel ruler, a carpenter's 1-foot-by-2-feet square, a pencil, a hobby knife and scissors. Cover the floor and the area beneath the dollhouse with newspapers, but to avoid ink smears, keep the newsprint away from the wallpaper and your hands.

Spray the printed side of the wallpaper with a light coat of clear flat acrylic paint. This seals the surface, reducing the chances of fingerprints or smudges marring the finish.

Fig. 13-3. Measure the height of the ceiling.

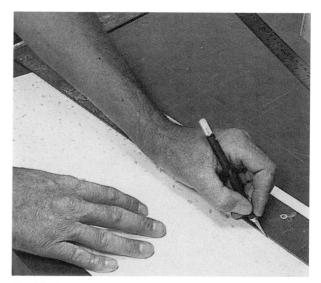

Fig. 13-4. Cut the wallpaper to match the ceiling height minus ⅛ inch.

COVERING THE CEILING

If you are going to wallpaper the ceiling, start there. The edges of the wallpaper must bend around each inside corner and run down the walls about ¼ inch. Measure the width and length of the ceiling and add ½ inch to each dimension.

Lay the wallpaper on your working surface and mark those dimensions on the back of the paper. Cut the paper to that size, and mark the precise dimensions of the ceiling on the paper. Hold the back edge of the paper under a steel ruler and fold the excess ½ inch upward, using the ruler to make a crease. Hold the paper against the ceiling to see if the crease is in the right place, producing a perfect corner along the joint between the front wall and the ceiling.

Turn the wallpaper facedown and apply the paste with the sponge brush. Work quickly, leaving no dry spots.

Press the still-wet paper onto the ceiling with the fold against the rear corner. Push the fold firmly into the corner between the wall and the ceiling. Using a massaging motion, spread the paper smoothly across the ceiling with your hands. Gently push the overlapping ¼ inch down the side walls, firmly pushing the wallpaper into the corners between the side walls and the ceiling. Let the paper bunch together in the two

rear corners. When it's firmly in all three corners, pinch the excess paper together in the corners and cut it out. Gently wipe over the edges with a damp sponge to remove any excess paste.

Move one of the lights so it casts shadows down the ceiling to see if there are lumps or bubbles in the wallpaper. If you spot any, use the hobby knife to make an X-shaped cut through the paper. Pull back the edges of the cuts and inject some wallpaper paste with the plastic syringe. Push the paper back down and use the sponge to wipe away excess paste.

MEASURING AND FITTING

Wallpapering really starts with the walls themselves. If the walls are perfectly square with the floor and with one another, the paper should go on easily. When you install the walls, check the corners with a carpenter's try square, a machinist's square or even an old book.

One method of wallpapering a dollhouse is to use a single piece of paper that wraps around all three walls without a seam. Few rooms are that small, so you'll have to piece the paper together with several sheets. Keep the one-piece concept in mind as you cut and fit the wallpaper.

Measure the width of the two side walls and the rear wall, and add those three dimensions

Fig. 13-5. Make sure the wallpaper will fit into the room.

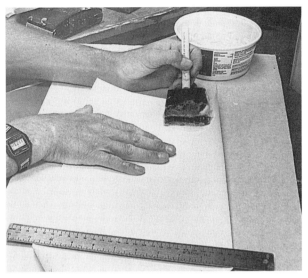

Fig. 13-6. Cover the back of the wallpaper with an even coat of wallpaper paste.

plus an inch. That's the length of the "single" piece of wallpaper.

Measure the height of the room and deduct ⅛ inch. (See Fig. 13-3.) That's the height of a single piece of wallpaper. The paper will stretch some when it's wet, and that ⅛ inch prevents the paper from extending beyond the bottom of the walls. Place the wallpaper faceup on the worktable and mark these dimensions lightly with a pencil and steel ruler. (See Fig. 13-4 and Fig. 13-5.)

ALIGNING REPEATING PATTERNS

If you need more than one piece of wallpaper, butt the second piece against the first and check to see if the repeating patterns align. If the top of both pieces face the same direction, the patterns will likely repeat. If they do not, overlap the papers until the patterns repeat correctly.

Hold a steel ruler tightly over the overlapping papers and use a hobby knife to slice through both layers. Try to make the cut along the edge of a pattern or printed line so it will be less obvious.

This technique assures a perfect match, and you don't have to reach into the room to try to make any cuts. Try the wallpaper in the room to see that it fits and that there's enough to cover

all three walls with at least an inch of excess length.

APPLYING THE PAPER

Turn the first sheet of wallpaper facedown on the work surface and apply the wallpaper paste with the sponge brush. Work quickly and be sure there are no areas without paste. (See Fig. 13-6.)

Hold the pasted paper against the wall, with the upper edge right along the ceiling. Start in the rear corner. Align the paper with the ceiling first, then gently crease it into the vertical corner between the side wall and the rear wall. Be sure any vertical patterns or lines are straight. Press the paper firmly into the corner. Gently push it against the wall, starting along the ceiling and working downward and outward toward the open face of the dollhouse. Use a gentle massaging motion to smooth the paper. Work the wallpaper around the edges of the window or door openings, and leave the paper alone until it dries.

Apply paste to the second piece. Hold this piece against the vertical edge of the first piece, and align the upper edges and the patterns. Work the paper along the edge of the ceiling, then spread it over the wall with that massaging motion. When you have worked the paper to the second vertical corner, press it firmly into

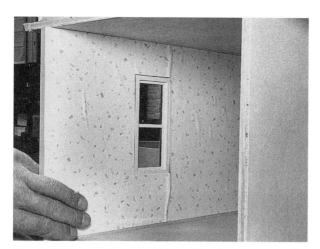

Fig. 13-7. Remove large bubbles while the paper is still wet by cutting a slit in the wallpaper and injecting more paste.

Fig. 13-8. Press the wallpaper against the walls and smooth it out. When it dries, run a fingernail down the edges of the windows and doors to mark their locations.

the corner from the direction of the back wall.

Finish by pressing the paper along the ceiling edge of the third wall and, finally, spreading it across the third wall. Let any excess paper hang off the edge of the wall until it dries.

Hold the light inside the room to check for lumps or bubbles. Slice an X-shaped cut into the bubbles, inject some wallpaper paste between the cut edges and push the wallpaper back down. (See Fig. 13-7.) Wipe over the area with a damp sponge to remove any excess paste.

Let the wallpaper dry for about two days, then use your fingernail to trace the outline of each window or door. (See Fig. 13-8.) Slice along those outlines with a hobby knife and remove the excess wallpaper. (See Fig. 13-9.) The frame of the window or door will hide any jagged paper edges. It's this simple because you have not yet installed the windows and doors.

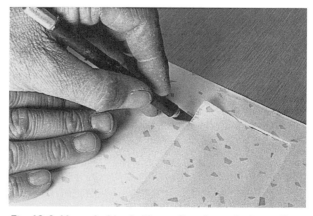

Fig. 13-9. Use a hobby knife to slice through the wallpaper around the window and door openings.

choose a decorative wallpaper for the lower portion of the wall and a plain paint or a simpler wallpaper pattern for the upper portion.

ADDING CHAIR RAILS AND WAINSCOTING

Walls with two colors are classic interior designs. The colors are usually separated by an ornate wood chair rail set between 24 and 36 inches from the floor. Northeastern Scale Models, Miniature House, Midwest and Real-Life Products offer milled-wood chair rails. You can

CHAIR RAILS

Pick a height for the chair rail, then measure the distance from the floor to the chair rail and make marks on the ends of the walls and beside any door or window. Use a pencil and ruler to connect the marks so you have a guideline for the chair rail. If you are going to paint above it, apply the paint and let it dry before marking the chair rail's position.

Fig. 13-10. This yet-to-be-opened country store features Northeastern Scale Models wainscoting, topped with a chair rail.

Cut the wallpaper into strips, just as you would for a full wall, but consider the chair rail to be the "ceiling." Remember to deduct ⅛ inch from the height of the chair rail to allow room for the wallpaper to expand. Apply the paper or paint before installing the chair rail. Stain or paint the chair rail before cementing it to the walls with clear silicone bathtub caulking compound.

WAINSCOTING

Wainscoting is an alternative to wallpaper for decorating the lower portion of a two-color wall. It's commonly seen in three styles: as sanded and varnished vertical boards, ornate milled-wood panels (similar to matching rows of blank picture frames) and ornate leaf or wreath patterns carved or cast into plaster.

Northeastern, Miniature House and Real-Life offer milled-wood wainscoting panels and matching chair rails. Cut the wood into strips the height of the chair rail with a razor saw, guided by a carpenter's try square. Stain or paint both sides of the wainscoting so it does not warp. Cement the wainscoting to the wall with Quick Grab Cement by 3C to minimize any chances of warping the thin wood.

Northeastern offers picture frame–style milled-wood wainscoting in four styles: 2³⁄₁₆ x 2³⁄₁₆-inch square, a set of three rectangles, two rectangles or six squares (stacked in two rows of three) in 2³⁄₁₆ x 3-inch sets. You'd need four sets for a 12-inch-long wall and a chair rail for the top. (See Fig. 13-10.) Miniature House has some similar rectangular wainscoting patterns, but with each corner cut into a concave circle.

The ornate cast-plaster wainscoting is available in several styles from Unique Miniatures. This is a cast-resin material that can be cut with a razor saw. Cut the wainscoting to the correct length, paint it and glue it to the wall with Quick

Grab cement. Use one of the ornate milled-wood mouldings from Northeastern, Miniature House or Midwest as a chair rail.

Some wainscoting merely stops at the floor, but most styles are used with some type of milled-wood baseboard. The baseboard is particularly useful in covering up any uneven bottom edges of the vertical board-style wainscoting.

FINISHING WINDOWS AND DOORS

It's finally time to install those exterior doors and windows. The techniques for aligning them and fitting them to walls that are too thin or too thick are described in Chapter 11. Stain or paint the trim and cement it to the walls with Tacky cement.

The interior doors may need modifications. All of the accessory doors include a lower sill. That's fine if the door is going to be used as an exterior door because those usually have a sill or threshold. Most interior doors in real houses, however, have no threshold. The techniques to modify the doors to remove the thresholds are described in Chapter 11.

ADDING CLOSETS

Closets are seldom included in dollhouses because they consume too much floor space.

There are add-on closets, complete with bifold louvered or paneled doors, available from Timberbrook. The closets are 1½ inches deep x 5⁵⁄₁₆ inches wide and are available in 7⅞-inch and 10-inch heights. The folding doors, with either louvers or panels, are sold separately so you can create built-in closets, too. There are also a number of freestanding closets or armoires available from dollhouse-furniture manufacturers.

PLANNING FOR RENOVATIONS

Remember that this is a dollhouse: a place where you can try out your whims or fantasies. You can experiment, too. Play with decors you'd never consider for your real home, such as unique color combinations and furniture you fancy. All of it can be changed as you desire. A dollhouse is a piece of cake to redecorate or even renovate, from foundation to attic.

If you are seriously considering a miniature makeover in a year or so, the windows and trim can be stuck in place with the sticky waxes such Mini-Hold, Hold or Blue Tack, sold by some art-supply stores. The wax will hold the components as well as any baseboards or ceiling covings and cornices, but the parts can be easily pried loose with a fingernail. It makes it a snap to repaint or change wallpaper.

CHAPTER FOURTEEN

CEILINGS, FLOORS AND TRIM

The interior decoration of your dollhouse isn't complete until you finish the ceilings and floors. The ceiling may already be covered with paint or wallpaper, unless you choose to use ornate-style ceiling panels. Finish the ceiling, including any crown cornices or coving trim, before installing the flooring, carpeting or baseboards. That way, you won't take the chance of accidentally dropping ceiling material onto your finished floor. Finally, you'll add the baseboards.

FINISHING THE CEILING

The ceiling's surface can be either painted or covered with wallpaper (described in Chapter 13), or you could go for a more elaborate look. Stamped metal tiles, found in some Victorian homes, are replicated in vacuum-formed and painted plastic panels from JR Enterprises. Some French and Italian Provincial houses had ceilings with cast or carved plaster wreaths and flowers. Those patterns are duplicated in cast resin from Unique Miniatures.

The edges of the ceiling can simply join the walls at angles or be embellished with milled-wood crown cornices or coving mouldings, ranging from simple concave half-circles to complex designs from Midwest, Northeastern Scale Models, Miniature House, Houseworks and Real-Life Products. Ornate carved flowers are available from Unique Miniatures.

Some real homes have a picture rail circling the room about a foot below the ceiling. You can create this look with chair rails from Midwest, Northeastern, Miniature House or Real-Life.

Use gold-plated jewelry chain to hang several miniature pictures from the rails.

The techniques to install baseboards, discussed later in this chapter, can be used to install crown mouldings, coving mouldings or chair rails. There's a photograph in the color section of a dollhouse interior with a finished ceiling that includes coving.

ADDING WOOD FLOORS

Houseworks, Handley House, Miniature House and others make hardwood flooring for dollhouses. The boards are perfect 1/12-scale replicas of the widths and even the patterns of real hardwood floors. Individual boards are supplied already assembled in 11 x 17-inch "gang-flooring" sheets, which can be installed as quickly and easily as the clapboard exterior finishing panels. The flooring, however, must be cut to fit the room precisely before it's glued in place.

If you want, flooring can be made from individual wood strips sold by Miniature House and Northeastern Scale Models. The advantage of this method is that you can create interesting patterns, such as stars, hexes or pyramid-pattern squares, to accent entryways or hearths. The strips are also useful for covering floors in rooms with odd or angled shapes. The boards from the gang-flooring panels can be removed and installed one at a time if you prefer a particular wood or size that's not readily available in individual strips.

Interior floors come in a choice of woods including plain oak, black oak, red oak, tan oak, pine, southern pine, walnut and American wal-

133

Fig. 14-1. J. Hermes sells printed papers to simulate hardwood flooring.

Fig. 14-2. Press a 6 x 8-inch sheet of paper into the corners below the bay window.

nut. Some are also available as conventional flooring-width boards, wider country-style boards and in herringbone, parquet and picture-frame patterns.

The lighter colors seem to work best in dollhouses. Most real floors are oak, although fir is common in the West and Midwest. For a miniature floor, cherry is a good choice because its fine grain appears more to be the proper scale than does some real oak. Cherry can also be stained to look like oak, or bleached and stained to look like fir.

Many turn-of-the-century homes, including Victorians and some early bungalows, have porch floors made from narrow interlocking tongue-and-groove flooring. That can be simulated using the Northeastern 370 milled-wood Scribed Siding sheets with ¼-inch-wide boards. Usually, these floors were painted, not stained or varnished.

If you want to economize, you can choose from several printed paper flooring patterns including wood flooring and tiles from J. Hermes and others. (See Fig. 14-1.) Use the techniques for installing wallpaper, described in Chapter 13, to apply paper flooring.

GANG-PANEL FLOORING

To put in gang-panel flooring, make a paper pattern that's the precise size and shape of the floor.

Start with any bay window, alcove or other odd-shaped area of the room. Take a piece of paper and push it tightly against the bottom corners of the walls. (See Fig. 14-2.) Make deep creases with your fingernail so the paper fits tightly into the area. Remove the paper and cut along the creases with scissors. Put the cutout piece back in place.

Place a second piece of paper in one corner and a third piece in the second corner, then tape them together. Add a fourth piece, tucked tightly into the third corner, and a fifth piece for the fourth corner. Tape them all together. (See Fig. 14-3.) This system will correct for any out-of-square corners.

Decide if you want the boards to run with the width or with the depth of the house. It's easiest to run them with the depth because you can piece the gaps in doorways with one or two loose boards. If you run the boards with the width, the boards that extend through the doorways must be spliced to fit the patterns of the boards in adjacent rooms. In that case, add another piece of paper to the pattern to extend the flooring into the next room for at least an inch. Do the same thing with the floors in adjacent rooms.

When you lay the flooring, cut the extra inch out of every other board of the overlapping flooring so there's a zigzag pattern across the doorway.

Fig. 14-3. Place four more sheets of paper into the room, one in each corner, and tape them together.

Fig. 14-4. Tape the paper pattern to the flooring and use a hobby knife or scissors to cut the wood along the edges of the pattern. Guide the knife with a steel ruler.

The finished pattern will look like the interlocking ends of vertical rows of bricks, except that the overlap is an inch and the "bricks" are 2 inches long. For more realism, vary the lengths of those interlocking boards.

If the room is larger than either the 11-inch or 17-inch dimension of the "gang-flooring" sheets, you will have to use a second piece of flooring. It's certainly easier to join flooring along the edges of boards than to join it end to end. However, you can use the interlocking brick technique to overlap the ends. Fit the two panels together in the way you choose so they will fit the paper patterns, and temporarily tape them together on the back side. Remove the tape just before you stick the flooring permanently into the room.

PAINTING AND FINISHING WOOD FLOORS

It's a lot easier to paint and finish (and even wax) the flooring before you cut it to fit the rooms. You'll be able to see the most remote corner as clearly as the portion that will be along the edge. You can use as much force as you wish to sand the surface and work right into and beyond what will be the corners.

The sheets are also easy to work with because of their large size. There's enough excess material to allow some unfinished edges

to hold on to. I suggest you make all the patterns for rooms that will use similar flooring. Place all of those patterns on the flooring so you can see which areas are scrap. Remember to run the flooring either with the length or depth of the rooms when you position the patterns. The unused areas can be left unfinished to serve as handles while you finish the flooring.

The techniques for staining wood are described in Chapter 7. Let the stain dry for at least two days. Use a high-quality ¾-inch-wide brush to apply three coats of Deft Semi-Gloss Clear Wood Finish or a similar clear semi-gloss polyurethane varnish. Let each coat dry, then sand the surface lightly with fine-grit sandpaper. Wipe the dust away with a damp rag. Do not sand the final coat. Let that dry for a day. Wax the floor with paste floor wax.

LAYING THE FLOORING

Read the instructions furnished with the wood flooring. Some brands suggest that you use an iron to heat the wood to bond it permanently to the paper backing. Here's an easier alternative: When the flooring is finished, apply a final coat of clear polyurethane semi-gloss varnish, which will bond the boards to the paper.

Tape the pattern to the top of the 11 x 17-inch piece of flooring. Use heavy scissors to cut

135

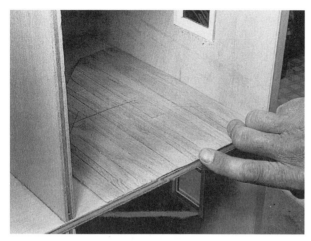

Fig. 14-5. Press the flooring down firmly onto the double-stick carpet tape.

through the thin wood and paper backing, cutting right along the edge of the paper pattern. (See Fig. 14-4 on page 135.) You can get a much more precise replica of the pattern with this system than the usual system of tracing the pattern onto the wood with a pencil. The baseboard mouldings will hide the slightly rough ends of the cut boards.

If there is the faintest chance you might want to remove the flooring to reach a tape wire or to redecorate, do not glue the flooring to the plywood. Instead, use double-sided carpet tape. (See Fig. 14-5.)

Run the tape along all the edges of the room. Lay a few more strips down the center to cover all but a few square inches of the floor. Cut the tape carefully so it doesn't ever overlap itself. A few empty square inches won't matter because the flooring is attached to its own paper backing.

Start with the flooring carefully aligned with one corner and gradually work it into the room. Do not attempt to gently lower it into place all at once or it will form humps that buckle and bow the wood. Work the flooring down firmly, using the same massaging motion with your fingers and hands that you used to install the wallpaper. (See Chapter 13.)

INSTALLING INDIVIDUAL BOARDS

The $\frac{1}{16}$ x $\frac{1}{8}$-inch wood strips are very close to exact-scale flooring for dollhouses. Real flooring

boards come in lengths ranging from about 3 to 8 feet. Use a miter box and razor saw to cut enough pieces to cover the floor. Remember that this is a pretty permanent floor.

If you choose individual boards for the flooring, lay them right on the plywood. If there are tape wires on the floor for a ceiling fixture in the room below, leave a few boards loose around the area where the wires for the fixture will be connected. If those loose boards are a bother, they can later be held in place with one of the sticky waxes like Hold or Mini-Hold.

Use Quick Grab Cement by 3C so the boards don't warp. Apply a bead of the glue and spread it with a tongue depressor so it is as wide as three or four boards. After you have laid two rows, add more glue for two more rows. This technique will keep the glue away from the already-laid boards. Work outdoors so you can quickly wipe away, with a rag and thinner, any cement that does reach the boards.

Start by laying all the boards needed to finish the first row along the outside edge of the room. Add the second row, more glue, then the third and fourth rows, more glue, and so on until the boards have reached the rear walls. Cut any boards to fit in angled areas, like bay windows, as needed.

Measure the gap between the last row of boards and the far wall. If the gap is more than $\frac{1}{8}$ inch, cut the boards to that width with a razor saw or sand the edges to fit. If the gap is less than $\frac{1}{8}$ inch, it can be covered with the baseboard mouldings.

The corners will be finished with baseboards. If the gap is $\frac{1}{16}$ inch or less, the baseboard will cover it. If it's $\frac{1}{8}$ inch or less, add one of the $\frac{1}{16}$-inch quarter-round strips to the baseboards.

INSTALLING TILE FLOORS

You can choose from several types of simulated tile floors for dollhouses. Individual tiles, glued to paper backing, are available from Handley and Miniature House. Tiles printed on smooth plastic sheets are produced by Eden Craft and What's Next? Vacuum-formed sheets of tiles, with the grouting in a recessed gap, are produced

Fig. 14-6. Use double-stick carpet tape to install the sheets of floor tiles.

by JR Enterprises, Precision and Miniature House. Miniature House also makes imitation marble panels. Tierney's Tiles produces real tiles in 1/12-scale.

Make a paper pattern of the exact shape of the room, as described earlier. Tape the pattern to the tiles and cut them out with heavy scissors. Use clear silicone bathtub caulking compound to install printed tiles, paper-backed loose tiles and vacuum-formed sheets. (See Fig. 14-6.)

Make a backing for the loose tiles from a piece of surgical gauze that's at least an inch larger than the paper pattern. Use a steam iron to flatten the gauze. Place the gauze over waxed paper.

Glue the tiles to the gauze with clear silicone bathtub caulking. Use 1/32 x 1/4-inch pieces of wood, placed on edge, as spacers between rows of tiles. Adjust the space between the tiles in each row by eye. Use end-nipper-style diagonal cutters or a hacksaw to cut the tiles to fit along the far walls or into angled corners. Remove the wood before the glue dries; allow the gauze and tiles to dry overnight.

Glue the sheet of tiles to the floor with clear silicone bathtub caulking and let it dry overnight. Using a spatula, spread spackling compound over the floor to fill the spaces between the tiles. With a damp rag, wipe excess compound from the faces of the tiles.

ADDING CARPETS AND RUGS

You'll find woven carpeting in 1/12-scale, but you can also use velour fabric for carpeting. Dozens of rugs, of every size and style, can simply be placed over hardwood or tile floors.

To install wall-to-wall carpets, make paper patterns as described earlier. Tape the patterns upside down to the bottom of the carpet. Woven dollhouse carpets have a grain like real carpets. If you are going to use the same carpet for more than one room, be sure that the grain is lying in the same direction in all rooms. If the carpet is too narrow for the room, add the extra pieces near the inside walls, and watch the direction of the grain.

Use double-sided carpet tape to install the carpets. The tape doesn't need to cover as much of the area as it does with hardwood floors; just cover all the edges of the rooms with the tape and place another strip every 6 inches across the center.

Press the carpet firmly onto the tape. The baseboards will disguise any jagged edges along the walls. If the carpet edge doesn't look finished enough, Houseworks, Handley and Northeastern make 1/4-inch and 3/8-inch channels that can be used to finish the outside edge of the floor.

As an alternative, you can use paper rugs. Look for books, with full-color illustrations of rugs, on sale for a few dollars. Cut out the color photographs to cover your dollhouse floors. Some dollhouse stores also carry printed paper rugs. Spray the paper with flat-finish clear paint, and touch up the edges with a black felt-tipped pen. Hold the carpets to the floor with a few dabs of Hold or Mini-Hold sticky wax.

INSTALLING BASEBOARDS

The baseboards are an interior detail that brings the dollhouse into the world of real houses in miniature. Northeastern, Midwest, Houseworks and Miniature House sell milled-wood baseboards in several styles. Northeastern and Midwest also have 3/32-inch quarter-round wood

Fig. 14-7. Hold the baseboard moulding in position and mark where to cut.

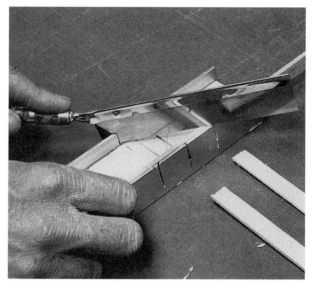

Fig. 14-8. Use a miter box and razor saw to make a 45-degree cut through the baseboard moulding.

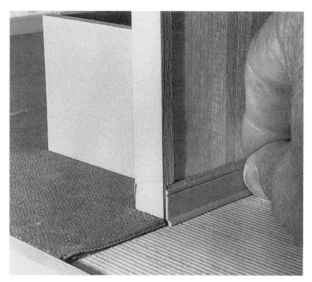

Fig. 14-9. Make 90-degree cuts where the baseboard meets door frames.

strips that can be used as baseboards in contemporary dollhouses or to extend the more ornate conventional baseboards in older-era dollhouses.

Stain or paint the baseboards as described in Chapter 7. Be sure to paint both sides so the wood does not warp.

Install the baseboards after all the window and door frames and the flooring or carpeting have been completed. Starting with one of the side walls, hold the baseboard in place and mark its length with a pencil. (See Fig. 14-7.)

Use a miter box and a razor saw that fits the miter box for all the cuts. Cut the baseboard about an inch longer than necessary, then insert the inside end into the miter box and cut it at a 45-degree angle to produce a mitered joint. (See Fig. 14-8.) Cut a similar baseboard for the opposite wall with a 45-degree mitered cut on the inner end. Hold the baseboards in place with Hold or Mini-Hold sticky wax.

Measure the exact distance between the inner ends of the baseboard. Cut a third piece that length plus ¼ inch. On one end of this piece, make a 45-degree miter cut to fit against one of the side wall baseboards. Hold the piece in place and mark precisely where to make the second 45-degree miter cut. Cut that end, then test-fit the baseboard.

You will be able to adjust for any slight misalignment in the mitered joints by moving one or two of the baseboards in or out. That's one of the reasons they're held in place with the sticky wax. When you're satisfied with the fit, mark where the outer ends of the two side baseboards are to be cut. Remove the two side baseboards and make a 90-degree cut so they're flush with the open sides of the dollhouse. (See Fig. 14-9.)

The 90-degree cut will have to be made, of course, where the baseboards touch any interior door mouldings. Use the same technique, but let the baseboard protrude into the door opening by that ¼ inch. Make the cut to fit the door opening the final cut.

Cement the baseboards in their original positions with clear silicone bathtub caulking compound. If you want to be able to remove the flooring to reach tape wires, put a piece of a business card between the baseboard and the flooring as you glue the baseboards in place. Remove the card to leave a slight gap.

Test-fit the baseboards along the edges of the carpeting. Some real carpets are covered with the baseboards, while other carpets cover the baseboards. Try it both ways to see which looks best in your dollhouse.

CHAPTER FIFTEEN

FURNITURE IN MINIATURE

Remember how you felt when you first walked into one of those massive warehouse marts full of real-size furniture? Hold on to that image of a hundred rooms full of furniture.

Now, imagine what that warehouse would have looked like in 1890, 1920, 1940 and 1960. What if you could turn back the clock and see all those finished rooms and that variety of furniture—all in one place?

You can. There is, literally, a warehouse full of 1/12-scale furniture, with appropriate wallpaper and floor coverings, window treatments, pictures, lamps and even the silver service, china, cookware, vases and bric-a-brac that you'd expect to see in a model home or a furniture showroom.

SHOPPING FOR MINIATURES

It would take a book five times this size to display all the choices. That book has yet to be published; even if it were, it would be out of date within weeks as more miniatures arrive on the market. The closest thing to that catalog is The Miniatures Catalog, 400 pages published every year or so by Kalmbach. Dollhouse dealers may also have Dee's Delights' 700-page catalog or Handley House's 500-page catalog. There's a lot of repetition between these three, but even they do not list all the products that are available.

Dozens, perhaps hundreds, of small manufacturers and dollhouse builders produce furniture, decor and accessories as well as custom shells and finished dollhouses for sale only in their local areas. That's why you'll find it so interesting to look for dollhouse dealers in every city you visit. Yes, the majority of their stock may be the same, but you are virtually guaranteed to find many items you've never seen and that have never been cataloged.

SELECTING A STYLE

There's a much wider choice of dollhouse furniture than of dollhouses. You can, for instance, buy Art Deco furniture as well as Egyptian-motif items, but don't expect to find matching dollhouses. There's furniture for every room including the kitchen and bathroom, from every era or period between about 1880 and today.

You have the option of selecting not only a style for furniture and interior decor but a period, with a choice of wood finishes and cloth patterns and colors. French Provincial furniture, for example, is available in mahogany, cherry and oak as well as hand-painted variations with ornate flowers and filigree.

Priscilla Washington finished the interior of Fantasy Craft's "Craftsman Bungalow," shown in Chapter 2. The kitchen cabinets are Fantasy Craft products. The upper cupboards have glass fronts made from acrylic plastic, and the flooring simulates linoleum. Although not visible in the photograph, glass-doored bookshelves flank a stone fireplace. The fixtures in the bathroom are replicas of some from the 1920s era; there's a footed bathtub and pedestal-style sink.

Fig. 15-1. Each piece of French Provincial furniture in this living room from Cameron's Collectibles is hand-painted.

You can decide if you want the interior and the exterior to match. Breathtaking realism is possible with such a coordinated dollhouse. Or, you can decorate the exterior in your favorite style and select a completely different look for the interior. You can even decorate each room with a different style or period. This is a dollhouse and it's all yours.

FURNISHING THE LIVING ROOM

For miniature living rooms, you can recreate anything from an Early American–style den that you might find in a 1970s split-level house (complete with shag carpeting) and Art Deco to wicker and Victorian designs. The Provincial living room shown in the photograph includes a number of hand-painted European miniatures. (See Fig.

15-1.) The scene is available as a complete room or as individual pieces from Cameron's Collectibles.

Consider four-posters, brass beds, bunks and cribs when decorating a bedroom. Four-poster bedroom sets can be purchased in half a dozen different styles, most with a choice of oak, mahogany or walnut woods. Some sets include the bed, night table, chest and dresser, but similar armoires and dressing tables and mirrors are also available. Wood, brass, trundle and bunk beds are made for dollhouses; so are various imitation iron-railing pieces.

Be sure to look for unusual hutches, glass-front china cabinets and accessories like tea carts for your dollhouse dining room. All of those items are on the shelves of larger dollhouse stores. If you want to leave out a formal dining room, you can pick up a breakfast nook, kitchen and patio chairs or table sets.

Fig. 15-2. This complete set of moderately priced appliances and furniture for a seventies-era kitchen is from Handley House.

STYLING KITCHENS AND BATHS

You can create a kitchen in any style. Oak ice-boxes and Hoosier-style glass-front cabinets and iron stoves characteristic of the 1880s are available from several manufacturers in different styles. You can also obtain matching sinks and cupboards. If you search a bit, you'll find replicas of early refrigerators with top-mounted coils, porcelain sinks and other kitchen furnishings typical of the 1920s and 1930s. Countertop ranges and hoods are also produced in l/12-scale, so you can create a modern kitchen with a peninsula-style counter, an appropriate sink and a double-door refrigerator.

The 1970s-era kitchen in the photograph is decorated with some of the least expensive furniture. (See Fig. 15-2.) The double-door refriger-

ator, stove, sink, table and four chairs are all included in the Handley House 90707 Kitchen Set.

This contemporary kitchen illustrates the selection of cupboards and details that are available. About two-thirds of the cupboards are included in the Pitty Pat Miniatures Modern Kitchen Grouping set. The set has been expanded with additional glass-front cupboards, a range hood, washer and dryer, kitchen stool, microwave oven, pots and pans, dishes and tableware, food, bags of groceries and a laundry basket full of dirty clothes. (See Fig. 15-3.) Similar details are offered by several other accessory manufacturers.

Dollhouse suppliers have created a virtual history of the bathroom. Precision Products has a vacuum-formed plastic kit to build a wooden outhouse. Turn-of-the century sinks as well as pitchers and basins are available. Cameron's

Fig. 15-3. These counters and cupboards are available as separate modular pieces from Pitty Pat Miniatures.

Fig. 15-4. The shower stall is simulated marble. The flower patterns on the fixtures are hand–painted in this quality furniture from Cameron's Collectibles.

Collectibles specializes in hand-painted European-style furniture. The Provincial bathroom scene, with mirrors on two walls and a footed tub, includes their exquisite products. (See Fig. 15-4.)

FURNISHING STORES, CHURCHES AND SCHOOLS

Expect the unusual. This hobby includes enough enthusiasts with a wide array of interests to make anything possible. There are, of course, furnishings for country stores—from the cash register to the counters and wrapping-paper dispensers. You can also purchase modern glass counters, clothing racks and other cabinets, and you'll find every imaginable type of food and food container. Thanks to the array of miniatures and full-color empty boxes that duplicate the boxes of contemporary plastic toys, a toy store is as easy to furnish as a country store.

There are also some surprises. Fantasy Craft makes church pews. And an altar could be adapted from an ornate dining-room hutch or even a much-modified fireplace. Several firms make small organs to finish the scene.

Fantasy Craft also makes benches for a country school interior, a chalkboard and a teacher's desk. Several firms provide children's books and toys. Search far enough and you will find everything from model kits and toy trains in their colorful boxes, to Barbie™ dolls and miniature dollhouses, to outdoor swing sets, playground equipment and even 1/12-scale outdoor playhouses.

CHAPTER SIXTEEN

LANDSCAPING

A dollhouse is one of the most lifelike of miniatures. The large scale makes it relatively easy to recreate the smallest detail from the real world. You've finished the exterior, perhaps even with a porch, rain gutters and downspouts, but isn't something missing? Of course. There's no yard.

WHERE TO CREATE A YARD?

For some of us, the fantasy ends too abruptly outside our dollhouse. The miniature home seems misplaced just sitting on a bare wood shelf. If only you could have a portion of the front lawn, garden, sidewalk or backyard, the scene would be more complete.

The question is, how much of a yard? When you discover that just about everything you'd find in a real backyard or front yard is available in l/12-scale, it may be difficult to decide on the size of that little "lot."

The limit will probably be the sheer size of the yard. Consider placing a relatively small yard around the dollhouse itself; say, 9 inches of front yard, a couple of inches on each side and 9 inches of backyard.

If you want a gazebo, hot tub, fish pond, vegetable garden, swing set, sandbox and lawn furniture, you'll need more space. You could squeeze all of those items on a backyard lot about 2 feet square, which can rest near the dollhouse.

Consider the house itself. If it's a conventional model, there's really no place for a backyard,

just the front and side yards. The front-opening dollhouses have a back wall, but it's blank. Are you willing to make a finished exterior rear wall just for a backyard? Or, are you willing to make a hinged back wall for a conventional dollhouse?

The most effective and practical method of adding a backyard is to consider it a side yard. There's usually plenty of shelf room to the side and you'd have no worry about adding a fourth wall. It would be nice to install a side door from the kitchen that would lead "outdoors," providing a visible excuse for the yard. There's an example of a dollhouse with a side yard in the color section.

BUILDING A DISPLAY PLATFORM

It's a good idea to build a platform for your dollhouse to rest on. That platform will become the base for any yard, and that's an esthetic advantage. On the practical side, it protects the edges of the dollhouse, especially porches and eaves, by providing a surrounding buffer or railing. When you want to move the dollhouse to another display table or shelf, the platform provides stable handles so you don't have to grab the foundation or porch.

There are limits to the size of a platform. First, it should be narrow enough so you can squeeze it through a 30-inch-wide door opening; 24 inches is a practical maximum width. The platform can be up to 8 feet long, but anything over 5 feet is difficult to maneuver. If you need 8 feet, you're probably considering a back (or side) yard. I suggest that you make the yard a separate platform. If the backyard is 24 inches square, that leaves 6 feet for the house, which should be plenty.

A 2 x 6-foot platform strong enough to support a dollhouse can be extremely heavy. Try to find a hollow-core door that size. Otherwise, build the platform with a ¼-inch plywood top, supported by a framework of 1 x 3 boards placed on edge. Attach the boards with drywall nails and carpenter's glue. This type of construction is best even for a platform as small as 2 x 3 feet.

If you want the platform to be really light, buy a ½-inch-thick Foamcore™ panel from a large art-supply store. It's made from plastic-coated cardboard surfaces with a Styrofoam interior. Support the Foamcore board with the same 1 x 3 wood frame. Protect the vulnerable edges with Houseworks or Northeastern Scale Models ½-inch milled-wood angle mouldings around all four edges.

SHAPING THE LANDSCAPE

The plywood or Foamcore panel is the surface that will be modified to simulate earth. If you're satisfied with a flat yard, it can be left alone. If you want some low hills or, perhaps, a fish pond, some additional construction is necessary.

Sloping hills can be carved easily from 1- or 2-inch-thick Styrofoam insulation board. Buy a single 4-foot-wide sheet, and use a serrated paring knife to cut it to fit the platform. Cement it to the platform with carpenter's glue.

Place the dollhouse on the Styrofoam. The dollhouse may sink into the Styrofoam ¼ inch or so. Wiggle the dollhouse a bit to push it as far into the Styrofoam as it's likely to go. Use a paint-roller handle to push the Styrofoam down around the edges of the dollhouse so the foundation is not partially hidden.

If you don't cover the platform with Styrofoam, you'll need to drill small holes to insert the stems or trunks for plants and trees. Use a ⅟₁₆-inch drill bit and an electric drill. Any place you see a reference to "pushing a nail or awl into the Styrofoam" in this chapter, just drill a ⅟₁₆-inch hole instead.

PLACING FISH PONDS AND SUNKEN GARDENS

You now have an "earth" yard that can be cut to create the bottoms of fish ponds. Use the paring knife to dig out a pond the size and shape you prefer. For inspiration, study the two photographs of fish ponds in the color section.

If you want a sunken garden, just slice through the Styrofoam down to the level of the plywood. Carve the edges into a gentle slope.

The leftover scraps of Styrofoam can be used to build up hills for a more interesting yard. There's a photo in the color section of just such a yard being finished beside a Duracraft "Lafayette" dollhouse. Use the paring knife to carve the 1-inch-thick Styrofoam into the general shape of the hills. Glue that piece to the yard with carpenter's glue and let it dry for a few days. Use the paring knife to carve gentle slopes into the side of that piece. If you want a slightly taller hill, glue on another, smaller piece of Styrofoam and carve it to shape.

PUTTING IN GRASS

Most of the Styrofoam or plywood yard will be covered with grass. The most realistic grass is a flocked paper made by Faller or Noch and sold to hobby dealers by Walthers. It combines several shades for a realistic, variegated effect and sticks up like real grass. A less expensive alternative would be the sawdust-covered "grass mats" available for toy trains. (See Fig. 16-1.)

If you want to simulate tall, unmown grass or weeds in some area of the yard, buy a piece of fake fur from a fabric shop. Dye it green or, for dead grass, light beige. Glue the cloth in place with clear silicone bathtub caulking.

ADDING SIDEWALKS

Use gray construction paper to test the locations of any sidewalks or paths. Cut the paper to the desired widths and shapes and lay the pieces on the grass. When you're satisfied with the locations, use a brown felt-tipped pen to mark the outlines of the sidewalks and paths on the grass. Slice through the grass with a hobby knife and remove the grass from the sidewalk areas.

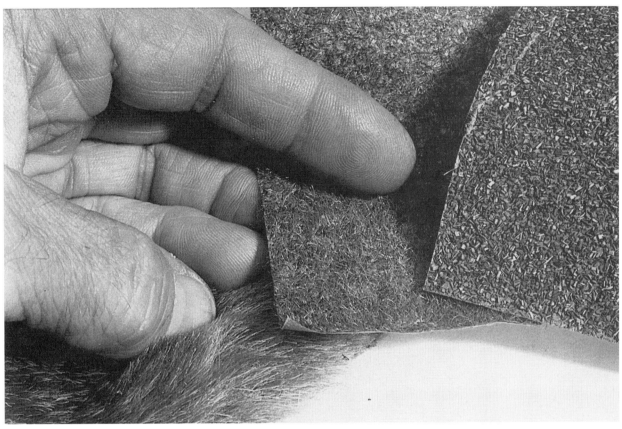

Fig. 16-1. Three alternatives for simulating grass include fake fur, Faller flocked paper and Life-Like Products' sawdust-covered paper mats.

To simulate concrete or blacktop, paint the area with Dee's Delights' Magic Stucco or Greenleaf's Dollhouse Stucco. Let the paint dry, then paint the surface a light yellow-gray to simulate concrete or a dark gray for blacktop. Use a black felt-tipped pen to draw any straight expansion joints or wiggly cracks on the concrete's surface.

Any of the simulated stone surfaces described in Chapter 6 can be used to create sidewalks or borders for gardens or ponds. Real flagstones are available from Timberbrook, or you can look for flat river rocks, slate or sandstone in the nearest woods.

CREATING FLOWER BEDS AND VEGETABLE GARDENS

Use brown construction paper to make test areas for gardens. Cut the paper to shape and rest it on the lawn where you think you will want dirt to be visible beneath flower or vegetable plants. Try different shapes and locations until you're satisfied, then trace the outlines with a brown felt-tipped pen. Cut through the grass and remove it.

Cover the areas that will be dirt with a thick layer of Artist's Matte Medium from an art-supply store. Sift dried real dirt through a flour sifter onto the wet Matte Medium. Gently press the dirt in with your fingers. Let the surface dry for at least a week, then use the hose of a vacuum cleaner to remove excess soil.

USING LIVE PLANTS

Some living plants can be used in the dollhouse garden; bonsai trees are the most obvious choice. The Styrofoam can be built up into a hill, then cut out to fit a pot containing a Bonsai plant.

Fig. 16-2. Simulate bushes by mounting dried weeds and flowers, and dyed greens in clumps of florist's clay.

Nursery stores can supply a number of small-leafed indoor plants for use as ground cover. For these, cut into the Styrofoam to form a small hollow to hold real dirt. Cover the hollowed-out area with a piece of brown plastic garbage bag. Using clear silicone bathtub caulking, glue the edges of the plastic to the Styrofoam, then add dirt and plants to the hollow. Keep live gardens to a minimum and water them carefully so there's no chance water will run across the "lawn" and into the dollhouse foundation.

Small ferns and other plants can be grown in the smallest clay pots, which are about the size of outdoor pots in 1/12-scale. Small potted cactus plants look great in a Southwestern yard.

Air ferns will grow just about anywhere and without water. Use a nail to push a hole through the grass and into the Styrofoam and just stick the stem of some air fern into the hole.

USING ARTIFICIAL SHRUBBERY

Imitation bushes and shrubs are the most common types of landscaping for dollhouses. Use dried green ferns to simulate small bushes or tiny trees. Stick these into small blobs of florist's clay, as shown on John Hutt's dollhouse scene, and place them around the dollhouse. (See Fig. 16-2.)

Life-Like Products and Heiki have ready-made trees intended for l/48-scale model railroads. (See Fig. 16-3 and Fig. 16-4.) They're relatively small for a dollhouse, but they may be large enough to suit you. A scale-size tree would be almost as big as the dollhouse.

Many of the scenery products and techniques used for model railroads can be used for dollhouses. Those techniques, including methods for making fall and winter scenes, are

Fig. 16-4. The Heiki trees are some of the largest available. The deciduous tree (left) is textured with ground foam, and the coniferous tree is textured with flocking.

Fig. 16-3. This Life-Like pine tree is a modified bottle brush with ground foam added to simulate clumps of pine needles.

described in my book *Scenery for Model Railroads, Dioramas and Miniatures* (Chilton Book Company, 1994).

One of the most common such products is lichen moss, which is treated and dyed by the manufacturer. Some of the Life-Like trees have plastic trunks with lichen moss branches and leaves. (See Fig. 16-5.) The lichen looks like what it is—moss. To make it look more like scale model leaves, cover the lichen with some of the green medium-size ground foam from AMSI or Woodland Scenics. Spray the lichen with Scotch Spray Mount (work outdoors), then dip it into a box lid full of the ground foam. (See Fig. 16-6

Fig. 16-5. Life-Like's trees have a plastic trunk, with lichen moss to simulate twigs and leaves.

Fig. 16-6. *Spray the clumps of lichen with Scotch Spray Mount to prepare them for a coating of ground foam.*

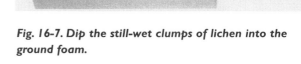

Fig. 16-7. *Dip the still-wet clumps of lichen into the ground foam.*

and Fig. 16-7.) Let it dry, then shake the excess foam back into the box.

Bits of ground foam look like leaves, so they're useful in simulating small plants in a vegetable garden.

Some dollhouse stores may carry scale model plants from firms like Robin's Roost. There's a wide selection of ferns and other leafy plants and flowers in pots. The pots can be removed and the plants placed in the outdoor garden. Push a hole through the grass and into the Styrofoam with an awl or nail and shove the stem of the plant into the Styrofoam.

SIMULATING TREES

Look for a dollhouse-size trunk and branch structure among the living plants around your house or in the woods. A tree about 15 to 18 inches tall is a good size for a dollhouse.

Push a 1½-inch-long nail into the base of the "tree" with pliers until just an inch of the nail is visible. (See Fig. 16-8.) Cut off the head of the nail with diagonal cutters. The nail will be used to support the tree in the Styrofoam.

Cover the tree with any of the materials that model railroaders use to simulate leaves. Clumps of lichen, covered with ground foam, is one choice. Woodland Scenics make a mesh covered with ground foam called Foliage Material, which suggests realistic small tree limbs with

Fig. 16-8. *Press a 1½-inch nail into the base of the tree trunk.*

leaves attached. The Foliage Material must be stretched until it is lacy. (See Fig. 16-9.) Use scissors to cut the material into clumps about 3 x 6 inches. Spread the clumps over the branches of the tree. (See Fig. 16-10.) The clumps will usually just hang where you put them. If you need to use glue, apply a dab of Artist's Matte Medium to the trunk and stick the Foliage Material to it. When you are satisfied, plant the tree by sticking that nail into the Styrofoam.

Some dollhouse stores sell custom-made trees and bushes. The trees, bushes, hedges,

Fig. 16-9. Pull the Woodland Scenics foam-covered Foliage apart until it looks lacy.

Fig. 16-10. Drape the Foliage over the tree trunk to simulate small twigs and leaves.

vines and flowers shown on the cover and in the garden scene in the color section are custom-made products from Creative Accents. This firm uses a combination of handmade tree trunks and limbs and dried plants to produce some very realistic landscaping.

CONSTRUCTING PONDS AND POOLS

It's possible to simulate a shallow fish pond on bare plywood. First, make a border or dam around the pond area with florists' clay. Insert a border into the clay with real stones or Miniature House's or Houseworks' real bricks or square tiles. The pond can certainly be deeper and more realistic if you cut it into a Styrofoam earth, as described earlier.

Paint the inside of the pond with at least four coats of flat interior latex wall paint. If it's an earthen pond, use an earth color. If the pond is supposed to be concrete, use a yellow-gray or one of the pastel colors that match the colors of dyed concrete. Let this dry for a week.

Mix some decoupage covering. This is a two-part clear resin. Buy the kind that uses equal parts of resin and catalyst in the mix. Do not use the type of resin or epoxy that requires only a few drops of resin with the catalyst, as it may not harden completely.

Mix the resin and pour it into the pond. Pour only enough to cover ¼ inch of the bottom and let it cure. Mix another batch and pour another ¼ inch into the pond. Repeat the process until the pond is full. If you attempt to pour more than that ¼-inch depth, the resin will likely crack as it cures.

If you want goldfish in your pond, shape them from orange Fimo clay. Put the goldfish into the pond after the first layer of resin cures, then submerge them with the second layer.

ADDING FENCES

Wood picket fences are available, ready to paint and install, from Houseworks, Handley, Builder's Choice and others. Cut vertical posts from ¼-inch-square wood. Make the posts a half-inch longer than the height of the fence. Sand the bottom third of each post until round. Drill ¼-inch holes in the plywood (or punch them in the Styrofoam with a bare drill bit). Cement the posts to the fence and paint the fence. Push the assembled fence and posts into the holes.

Wrought-iron fencing is available, molded in plastic, from Nash Wholesale and Lawbre. Laser-cut wood, which can be painted to look like wrought iron, is available from Laser Tech. You can cut fence posts from wire coat hangers with diagonal cutters. Paint the posts black to match the fence, then push them into the Styrofoam. Attach the fence to the posts with clear silicone bathtub caulking compound.

ADDING GAZEBOS AND GARDEN SEATS

There are a number of gazebo kits available from Houseworks, Betty's Wooden Miniatures, Carlson Miniatures (American Craft Products), Dee's Delights and others. You can put these kits together using the techniques described for assembling porches in Chapter 10.

There are a few kits to build garden seats or arbors. Greenleaf Products has two, and you may find some, made by local craftspersons, at dollhouse stores.

Norm Nielsen made the gazebo shown in the color section using pre-fabricated wood lattice-work from Handley House. Miniature House, Miniature Lumber Shoppe and Timberbrook also make preassembled latticework. The framework was assembled from $\frac{1}{8}$ x $\frac{1}{4}$-inch Northeastern wood with two porch posts to support the front. A friend made the simulated cast-concrete bench. Benches with simulated wrought-iron ends and wood slats for supports are available from Lawbre and others.

The vines on the side and roof of the seat are from Creative Designs. The Woodland Scenics Foliage Material would make a realistic substitute for vines.

GLOSSARY

addition. One or more rooms added to one or both sides of a dollhouse to increase the interior space. Sometimes called a wing or extension.

apex. The area beneath the peak of a roof.

baseboard. The strip of wood, often ornate, covering the joint between the wall and the floor or carpet.

bay window. An alcove or window that extends beyond the outer face of the walls.

board and batten. Wood exterior walls constructed from vertical boards. The gaps between the boards are covered with thin strips of wood.

bracket. The support for a shelf or overhanging roof.

butt. To join edge to edge, with no overlap.

candleflame bulb. A bulb that flickers to resemble a burning candle.

casement. A window style with a sash that opens by swinging on hinges, usually mounted on the side of the sash.

chandelier. The support for a number of lights mounted on a single hanging light fixture.

circuit. The path of a wire or tape wire that can be followed by an electrical current.

circuit breaker. An electronic device that automatically turns off the current when a short circuit occurs.

clapboard. A type of siding or covering using horizontal boards. Each board overlaps the top edge of the board below.

components. The windows, doors, trim and other accessories to finish a bare plywood dollhouse shell.

component set. A boxed set of all the windows, doors and other parts to finish a specific dollhouse.

corbel. A bracket, usually of wood or stone, that projects from the wall to support the edge of a roof or some other architectural element.

cornice. The overhang of a pitched roof.

cove moulding. A moulding, with a concave shape, used to finish inside corners of floors or ceilings.

current. The movement of electricity through wires or tape wires.

dentil. A style of ornate trim with rows of small rectangular blocks.

die-cut. The mass-production process used to slice through wood, cardboard or plastic.

dormer. A projection with three walls, built out from a sloping roof. The face usually has a window.

downspout. The pipe that carries water from the gutters on the edges of the roof to the ground.

drop siding. *See* **novelty siding**.

eaves. The extreme or outer edges of the roof, usually overhanging the walls.

embellishment. Something added to make the original object appear more ornate.

extension. *See* **addition**.

facade. The front of a building.

facia. A finishing board usually located along the

eaves or cornices to cover the edges of the roof.

false front. A front wall or facade that extends upward beyond the roof line to make the building appear larger.

finial. An ornament at the peak or top of a roof or piece of furniture.

fishscale. Shingles with rounded ends that resemble scales of fish when the roof is completed.

flashing. Sheet metal or plastic, usually used to protect areas where two portions of a roof join or where a chimney enters the roof.

flush. Level with surrounding surfaces, presenting a smooth and even surface.

front opening. A type of dollhouse design that has all four walls. The front is designed to be removed or is hinged so it can be opened.

gable. The apex of the roof, usually when two or more sets of sloping roofs are present.

gingerbread. Ornate and complex trim, usually beneath the eaves.

glazing. The glass in windows. It is usually clear plastic in dollhouse windows, but glass microscope slide material can be cut to replace the plastic.

grout. Cement or plaster, mixed thin enough so it will flow between bricks or tiles.

gutter. A shallow channel that's set along the horizontal eaves to carry rainwater to a downspout, channeling the water away from the walls and the foundation.

hip roof. A roof that rises at an angle from all four sides of a building. It usually has a flat top.

jamb. Usually, the side and top framework of a door that are closest to the door.

junction splice. Cir-Kit Concept's term to describe the plug-in connector that adapts conventional round wires to the tape wire system.

landing. The platform between two flights of stairs or at the top of a flight.

lath and plaster. A type of interior plaster wall construction used on real houses. The framework is covered with thin boards (called laths) with gaps between them that are filled with plaster.

lattice. An ornate wood covering made from pieces of thin wood or laths, which cross over each other to make a checkerboard pattern with square or diamond-shaped openings.

lintel. The piece of wood, stone, concrete or brick across the top of a window opening that supports the wall above.

mantel. The shelf above a fireplace.

miter. The joint between two pieces of wood where the joining ends are cut at an angle half that of the actual junction. A common window frame might have the ends of the joining boards cut at 45-degree angles to produce a 90-degree corner.

miter box. A channel-shaped device used to hold a piece of wood and guide the saw blade. Slots across the channel guide the blade to make accurate miter or square-end cuts.

molding. *See* moulding.

Monojet. *See* syringe.

moulding. Wood strips with curved or projecting surfaces. Used to finish or decorate inside and outside corners or to embellish walls.

mullion. Usually, the vertical bar or divider between windows. Sometimes used to describe equal-size vertical dividers.

muntin. Smaller vertical bars or dividers that are used inside areas bounded by window frames and mullions. The diagonal dividers that produce the diamond-shaped windows in some Tudor-style windows are muntins.

novelty siding. Wood exterior siding with horizontal boards butted together. Milled notches in both boards interlock to allow the top board to effectively overlap the bottom one, limiting the entry of rainwater.

O-scale. A dollhouse that is $\frac{1}{48}$ the size of the matching real house. The term is used by model railroad hobbyists to described similar-size trains. *See also* **scale**.

Palladian. A classic window and trim style with a half-circle placed over the top center of the window or trim.

parquet. A design or pattern of small pieces of wood, usually used in flooring.

pillar. The vertical support for a porch roof. Sometimes called a spindle.

pitch. The slope of a roof.

Playscale™. Trade name for Real Good Toys' dollhouses designed for Barbie™-type fashion dolls. The houses are built to a scale larger than 1/12 so the ceilings and door heights match the height of the dolls.

post. The vertical member of a decorative railing on a porch, stair or balcony. Sometimes called a spindle. *See also* **pillar**.

power strip. The term Houseworks uses to describe the terminal blocks for their plug-in system of conventional or round wiring for dollhouses. An insulated piece of plastic with sockets connects to a single pair of wires, much like an extension cord with a 12-plug capacity.

ridge. The peak of a roof, or the piece of trim sometimes placed along the ridge of a roof.

round wire. Conventional electrical wire. Used to differentiate between conventional wires and the copper strips in the tape wire system.

scale. The proportion of a model or miniature compared to the real thing, usually expressed as a fraction. Most dollhouses are $\frac{1}{12}$ the size of real houses.

shake. Thick shingles made by splitting, rather than sawing, the wood.

shell. A dollhouse, usually of bare plywood, that has no exterior or interior finishing, no shingles or other roofing, and no windows or doors.

shiplap siding. *See* **clapboard**.

shoe moulding. A baseboard moulding with a piece of quarter-round wood at the bottom.

siding. The final covering for exterior walls, usually made of wood or plastic or of metal shaped to look like wood.

soffit. The underside of an overhanging roof cornice.

splice. To join two pieces of wood so the joint is not visible; or to join two pieces of electrical wire or tape wire together so the current continues to flow across the joint.

syringe. A small hand-operated pump used to force fluid into a pin-size hole; sometimes used to apply glue when assembling and finishing dollhouses.

tape wire. The electrical wiring system used for some dollhouses, in which two strips of copper foil are bonded to self-adhesive tape. The tape is run from the transformer to the lights to carry the 12-volt electrical current.

threshold. The piece of wood across the bottom of a door opening.

transformer. An appliance that converts household 115-volt AC electrical current into 12 to 18 volts of DC current. Used to supply electrical current to lights.

vacuum-formed. A manufacturing process used to emboss designs or patterns on sheets of plastic, producing three-dimensional shingles, bricks, stones and wood siding. The shape and textures of the original master patterns are captured in the surface of the plastic sheet.

window treatment. Curtains, drapes, shades, blinds and surrounding decorations on windows.

wings. *See* **addition**.

SOURCES OF SUPPLY

When writing to any of these firms, enclose a self-addressed stamped envelope if you expect a reply. Some sell catalogs for a fee.

Alessio Miniatures
19 Everest Court
Huntington Station, NY 11746

American Craft Products
1530 Old North Rand Road
Wauconda, IL 60084

AMSI
P.O. Box 750638
Petaluma, CA 94975

Badger Air-Brush Co.
9128 Belmont Avenue
Franklin Park, IL 60131

Bespaq Corporation
200 Valley Drive, No. 37
Brisbane, CA 94005

Betty's Wooden Miniatures
6150 Northwest Highway
Chicago, IL 60631

BH Miniatures (see Dee's Delights)

Bill Lankford Creative Accents
3531 Beau Brummel
Amarillo, TX 79121

Builder's Choice (see New England Hobby Supply)

Cameron's Collectibles
171 A Hague Boulevard
Glenmont, NY 12077-3617

Carlson Miniatures (see American Craft)

Cir-Kit Concepts, Inc.
407 14th Street NW
Rochester, MN 55901

Clare-Bell, Inc.
P.O. Box 218
Lovell, ME 04051

Deco Art Americana (see Dee's Delights)

Dee's Delights, Inc.
3150 Stateline Road
North Bend, OH 45052-9731

Dragonfly International
6643 32nd Street, No. 106
North Highlands, CA 95660

Duracraft (available in toy, craft and discount stores)

Eden Craft (see Dee's Delights)

Elect-A-Lite (see Greenleaf Products)

Faller (see Wm. K. Walthers)

Fantasy Craft
933 Carson Lane
Pomona, CA 91766
909-591-8252

Fimo (see Dee's Delights or Handley House)

Floquil-Polly S. Corp.
Route 30
North Amsterdam, NY 12010

Grandt Line Products
1040 B Shary Court
Concord, CA 94518

Greenleaf Products, Inc.
P.O. Box 388, 58 N. Main St.
Honeoye Falls, NY 14472-0388
1-800-847-2545

Handcraft Designs, Inc.
63 East Broad Street
Hatfield, PA 19440

Handley House
2 Fourth Street
Wheeling, WV 26003

Heiki (see Portman Hobby)

Holgate and Reynolds
1000 Central Avenue
Wilmette, IL 60091

Houseworks, Ltd.
2388 Pleasantdale Drive
Atlanta, GA 30340

J. Hermes Miniatures
9609 Las Tunas Drive
Temple City, CA 91780

JR Enterprises
53 Case Road
Port Jervis, NY 12771-9442

Laser Tech
6669 Peachtree Industrial Boulevard, No. G
Atlanta, GA 30092

Lawbre (see Handley House)

Life-Like Products, Inc.
1600 Union Avenue
Baltimore, MD 21211

Lolly's
1054 Dundee Avenue
Elgin, IL 60120

Manorcraft Designs, Inc.
1813-B York Road
Timonium, MD 21093

Maureen O'Donnell (see Norm's Dollhouse)

Midwest Products Co., Inc.
P.O. Box 564
Hobart, IN 46342

Miniature House (see Dee's Delights or Handley House)

Miniature Lumber Shoppe
812 Main Street
Grandview, MO 64030

Mini Graphics
2975 Exon Avenue
Cincinnati, OH 45241

Nash Wholesale (see Handley House)

New England Hobby Supply
71 Hillard Street
Manchester, CT 05040-3001

Noonmark (see Dee's Delights)

Norm's Dollhouse
8227 South Holly
Littleton, CO 80122

Northeastern Scale Models, Inc.
P.O. Box 727
Methuen, MA 01844

Oakridge Corporation
P.O. Box 247
Lemont, IL 60439

Pitty Pat Miniatures, Inc.
1500 Old Deerfield Road
Highland Park, IL 60035

Plastruct, Inc.
1020 South Wallace Place
City of Industry, CA 91748

Polyterrain
HC 66, Box 93
Witter, AR 72776

Portman Hobby Distributors
P.O. Box 251
Peekskill, NY 10566

Precision Products
763 Cayuga Street, Unit No. 2
Lewiston, NY 14092-1724

Quality Shoppe (The)
212 S. Michigan Avenue
South Bend, IN 46601

Real Good Toys
10 Quarry Hill
Barre, VT 05641
802-479-2217

Realife Products (see Handley House)

Robin's Roost (see Dee's Delights)

Tierney's Tiles
8031 Tierney's Woods Curve
Bloomington, MN 66438

Timberbrook Wood Products
Hovey Lane
South Berlin, NY 13843

Unique Miniatures (see Dee's Delights)

Walmer Dollhouses
2100 Jefferson Davis Highway
Alexandria, VA 22301-3102

What's Next?
1000 Cedar Avenue
Scranton, PA 18505

Wm. K. Walthers, Inc.
P.O. Box 18676
Milwaukee, WI 53218

Woodland Scenics
P.O. Box 98
Linn Creek, MO 65052

PUBLICATIONS

CATALOGS

Dee's Delights, Inc.
3150 Stateline Road
North Bend, OH 45052-9731

Handley House
2 Fourth Street
Wheeling, WV 26003

Kalmbach Publishing Company
21027 Crossroads Circle
Waukesha, WI 53187

MAGAZINES

Dolls House World
Bimonthly; sample copy, $6.00
Heritage Press
3150 State Line Road
North Bend, OH 45052

Miniature Collector
Bimonthly; sample copy, $3.95
Scott Publications
30595 Eight Mile Road
Livonia, MI 48152-1798

Nutshell News
Monthly; sample copy, $3.50
Kalmbach Publishing Company
21027 Crossroads Circle
Waukesha, WI 53187

INDEX